HEALING from CHURCH HURT

To: Molly
Thank for helping me get better.
God bless you.

BISHOP RONALD R. MAYO PHD

HEALING
from CHURCH
HURT

Healing from Church Hurt
by Bishop Ronald R. Mayo, PhD

© 2017, Bishop Ronald R. Mayo, PhD
www.bishopronaldmayo.com
rise_2@hotmail.com

Published by Anointed Fire™ House
www.anointedfirehouse.com
Cover Design by Anointed Fire™ House

ISBN-10: 0-9982507-9-1
ISBN-13: 978-0-9982507-9-3

This book contains material protected under International and Federal Copyright Laws and Treaties. Any unauthorized reprint or use of this material is prohibited. No part of this book may be reproduced or transmitted in any form or by any means, electronic or mechanical, including photocopying, recording, or by any information storage and retrieval system without express written permission from the author/publisher.

I have tried to recreate events, locales and conversations from my memories of them. In order to maintain their anonymity in some instances I have changed the names of individuals and places, I may have changed some identifying characteristics and details such as physical properties, occupations and places of residence.

Some names and identifying details have been changed to protect the privacy of individuals.

Some of the stories in this book are fictional. Names, characters, businesses, places, events and incidents are either the products of the author's imagination or used in a fictitious manner. Any resemblance to actual persons, living or dead, or actual events is purely coincidental.

Although the author and publisher have made every effort to

ensure that the information in this book was correct at press time, the author and publisher do not assume and hereby disclaim any liability to any party for any loss, damage, or disruption caused by errors or omissions, whether such errors or omissions result from negligence, accident, or any other cause.

Scripture quotations, marked NIV are taken from The Holy Bible, New International Version ®, NIV ®, Copyright 1973, 1978, 1984, 2001 by Biblica, Inc.™ Used by permission. All rights reserved.

Scripture quotations, marked NLT are taken from The Holy Bible, New Living Translation, Copyright© 1996. Used by permission of Tyndale House Publishers, Inc., Wheaton, Illinois 60189. All rights reserved.

Scripture taken from the NEW AMERICAN STANDARD BIBLE®, Copyright ©1960,1962,1963,1968,1971,1972,1973,1975,1977,1995 by The Lockman Foundation. Used by permission.

Scripture quotations marked ESV are taken from The Holy Bible, English Standard Version®. English Standard Version are registered trademarks of Crossway®.

Table of Contents

Introduction IX

Are You Planted or Buried? 1

Church Culture 15

Hurt from the Door 23

Did You Check the Fruit? 33

Serving Laban 41

The Position of Offense 59

Top Five Reasons for Church Hurt 67

Gossip in the Church 79

Slandered by a Former Church 91

The Church Hurt Epidemic 99

Understanding Each Body 115

Common Reasons for Church Hurt 125

Unrealistic Expectations 145

The Concept of Marriage 163

The Taste Test 173

A Look at Trauma 191

Drive Them to Their Needs..205

A New Perspective..219

Understanding Measures...231

Healing from Church Hurt...243

Introduction

The term "church hurt" is still a relatively new term used to describe hurt, offense or trauma that has taken place between two believers. In most cases, both believers are a part of the same church body, with one of the believers being the leader and the other being a member. Of course, church hurt can and does occur between two or more members, just as it can occur between two or more leaders. Nevertheless, the majority of church hurt allegations come from members who've been hurt, offended or even traumatized by their leaders.

Church hurt is a very real problem, especially in this generation. Many leaders choose not to address the topic of church hurt, fearing that people who simply did not get their way will join the ranks of people who were truly hurt by the church, and amazingly enough, this is not far from the truth. There are people who've genuinely been done wrong, and then, there are people who simply didn't get what they wanted or expected from the church. These people have labeled their offense as "church hurt" and took up a cause against the church.

Before we get started, I want you to prepare yourself for what you're about to read. My goal isn't to help you point fingers because if I did that, you wouldn't heal properly. For example, if a bone is dislocated and the doctor does not put it back in place, the bone will begin to heal, but it won't heal properly. This would only make the dislocated limb malfunction and it would cause you much pain. To make matters worse, your doctor would likely have to perform surgery to properly relocate the bone and keep you from tearing a ligament. So again, my job isn't to bandage the wound; my job is to help you to see your own wounds from a surgeon's point of view. Did you really experience church hurt or were you just offended? The answer to this question makes a world of difference in the healing process. With that being said, as you navigate through this book, you'll find yourself having to do a lot of self-examination, as well as learn some of the most common reasons people experience church hurt in the first place.

This book isn't for victims who want to remain victims; it's for mature Christians who want to do more than go past the offense; they want to grow past it.

Are You Planted or Buried?

Many people have been wounded in the church, and for this reason, many have left the church altogether; some have even turned from the faith. Wounds compel us to react, and the sound of our reactions will either reflect the depth of our wounds or the height of our maturity level. Nevertheless, before we go charging into the topic of church hurt, we need to address whether you're currently or were planted in the church that hurt you or were you buried there? Understand this: you are a seed and the place you go to worship the Lord is your garden. You are a tree and what comes from your heart is the fruit you've been producing; it is the evidence of what you've been watering yourself with. Nevertheless, most people don't realize this, but a seed can be planted or it can be buried. If you plant a seed, it will produce after itself, but if you bury it, it will die.

When God comes looking for you, He comes looking for the fruit you are bearing or the fruit you were supposed to be bearing. If you're in the right church body, there should be fruit for Him to pick from, but if you're in the wrong church body, the fruit that will grow up for Him to examine will not be godly. Instead, it will be what the bible refers to as the fruit of the flesh.

The parable of the talents is an interesting story. It details the journeys of three men who had been given talents by their master. They all have the same master; this story was written this way because Jesus is our one and only master, plus, if the story involved three masters, most readers would resolve in themselves that the man who had one talent simply had a mean master. Howbeit, they had the same master and the same opportunity, only, they didn't have the same amount of talents. This is because the master granted each man a talent in accordance with his maturity. The story is in Matthew 25:14-30 (ESV) and it reads, "For it will be like a man going on a journey, who called his servants and entrusted to them his property. To one he gave five talents, to another two, to another one, to each according to his ability. Then he went away. He who had received the five talents went at once and traded with them, and he made five talents more. So also he who had the two talents made two talents more. But he who had received the one talent went and dug in the ground and hid his master's money. Now after a long time the master of those servants came and settled accounts with them. And he who had received the five talents came forward, bringing five talents more, saying, 'Master, you delivered to me five talents; here, I have made five talents more.' His master said to him, 'Well done, good and faithful servant. You have been faithful over a little; I will set you over much. Enter into the joy of your master.' And he also who had the two talents came forward, saying, 'Master, you delivered to me two talents; here, I have made two talents more.' His master said to him, 'Well done, good and faithful servant. You have been faithful over a little; I will set you over much. Enter into the joy of your master.' He also who had received the one talent came forward, saying, 'Master, I knew you to be a hard man, reaping where you did not sow, and gathering where you scattered no seed, so I was afraid, and I went and hid your talent in the ground. Here, you have what is yours.' But his master answered him, 'You wicked and slothful servant! You knew that I reap where I have not sown and gather where I scattered no seed? Then you ought to have invested my money with the bankers, and at my coming I should have received what was my own with interest. So take the talent from him and give it to him who has the ten talents. For to everyone who has will more be given, and he will have an abundance. But from the one who has not, even what he has will be taken away. And cast the worthless servant into the outer darkness. In that place there will be weeping and gnashing of teeth.'"

The first two servants produced fruit. When the master came to check on them, they showed him that they'd been utilizing the talents he'd given them and they had fruit to prove it. Howbeit, the wicked servant had nothing to show but the same talent that the master had given him. He'd buried his talent and by doing so, he dishonored his master.

Have you been planted in the right garden? What will you have to show when the Lord finds you? We all know the story of Adam and Eve and how they sinned against God, thus, causing the fall of humanity. Many theologians have taken a stab at dissecting the story in their attempts to determine what would cause a couple who had absolutely everything, to throw it all away just to sample a forbidden fruit. Genesis 2:15-17 gives us the backdrop of Adam and Eve's story. It reads, "The LORD God took the man and put him in the garden of Eden to work it and keep it. And the LORD God commanded the man, saying, "You may surely eat of every tree of the garden, but of the tree of the knowledge of good and evil you shall not eat, for in the day that you eat of it you shall surely die" (ESV). As we all know, Satan made his way into the Garden and contradicted what God said. He deceived Eve by simply sowing doubt in her heart. Genesis 3:1-13 reads, "Now the serpent was more crafty than any other beast of the field that the Lord God had made.

He said to the woman, "Did God actually say, 'You shall not eat of any tree in the garden'?" And the woman said to the serpent, "We may eat of the fruit of the trees in the garden, but God said, 'You shall not eat of the fruit of the tree that is in the midst of the garden, neither shall you touch it, lest you die.'"

But the serpent said to the woman, "You will not surely die. For God knows that when you eat of it your eyes will be opened, and you will be like God, knowing good and evil." So when the woman saw that the tree was good for food, and that it was a delight to the eyes, and that the tree was to be desired to make one wise, she took of its fruit and ate, and she also gave some to her husband who was with her, and he ate. Then the eyes of both were opened, and they knew that they were naked. And they sewed fig leaves together and made themselves loincloths." (ESV).

I'm not going to dissect this story, but I want you to take something from it — Adam and Eve were branches of righteousness in a well-watered garden. All of their needs were met and they weren't dealing with any bill collectors, student loans or vindictive exes. They had a life far better than the American dream, but they didn't know the value of what they had. For this reason, they sinned against God.

When God came looking for them, they were hiding, meaning, they weren't where they were supposed to be. Instead, they'd taken a few fig leaves and made grass skirts to cover their loins. They didn't bear the fruit (faith) needed to sustain them, and for this very reason, they were no longer allowed to inhabit the Garden of Eden. They were branches of a different tree now covering themselves with fig leaves. This means that they were no longer bearing the godly fruit of obedience.

Jesus's encounter with the barren fig tree is symbolic of God's encounter with Adam and Eve. Remember, Adam and Eve took fig leaves from a fig tree, but here it is that Jesus is on His way back to Bethany and He finds Himself hungry. He spots a fig tree and walks over to it. Matthew 21:18-19 tells the story this way, "In the morning, as he was returning to the city, he became hungry. And seeing a fig tree by the wayside, he went to it and found nothing on it but only leaves. And he said to it, "May no fruit ever come from you again!" And the fig tree withered at once" (ESV). What just happened here? Jesus came in contact with a fig tree — a tree that should have borne fruit, but for whatever reason, it was barren. When Jesus cursed the fig tree, He was pretty much removing God's blessing from it.

Without God's blessing, the tree could not survive. The same is true for mankind — we need God's blessing to survive and when He removed His blessing from us, He gave us another blessing called grace. This would allow us to live outside of the Garden of Eden, but it would not restore us to God. We needed a Savior; for this reason, Jesus Christ came into the earth.

Of course, we all know the story of Jesus's life, death and resurrection, but interestingly enough, when the Jews decided to crucify Jesus, they hung Him on a tree. Acts 5:30 reads, "The God of our fathers raised Jesus, whom you killed by hanging him on a tree" (ESV).

We keep seeing a reference to fruit in the biblical text. First, Eve eats the forbidden fruit and gives some to her husband. For this reason, they were sent out of the Garden of Eden and death entered mankind. Next, the Lord, Jesus Christ, comes across a fig tree on His way to Bethany and finds the tree not bearing any fruit. For this reason, He cursed the tree and it withered up. After this, we find that Jesus is hung on a tree and killed, and lastly, the Bible references the fruit of the flesh versus the fruit of the Holy Spirit. So, as you can see, God talks a lot about gardens, branches and fruit.

Your church home is your garden; it is the place that either you have planted yourself in or God has planted you in. It is a place where you are supposed to grow, flourish and produce fruit. It is a place where you're supposed to be covered (in prayer), taught and watered. But what happens when the church that was supposed to grow us begins to hinder us? What happens when we uproot ourselves from our church homes? The answer is simple — we experience what we now reference as "church hurt."

Think about a weed that's growing in your yard. Your grass is low, but a wild weed has suddenly shot up and it's about two feet tall. You walk over to the weed and step on it, breaking it in half. You have successfully killed the plant — the stem, that is. Nevertheless, the root is still in the ground. This is very similar to what happens when we experience church hurt. Someone breaks us in the place that we have rooted ourselves in, and despite our many attempts to move on with our lives, our roots prevent us from going too far. This is the pain we experience when we have been wounded in the church.

Church hurt can occur on many levels. For example, it can be two or more leaders who've either hurt or offended one another. It can be two or more congregants who have hurt or offended one another, and then again, it can be a leader and a congregant who has hurt or offended one another. What you'll find is that the most commonly reported church wounds are the results of leader/congregant relationships that have soured. This means that the man or woman who's acting as the farmer of a particular body of members has crushed one of the flowers that were growing up under his or her care. And it goes without saying that there are a host of reasons that some leaders do this. One of the most common reasons is — some leaders identify certain members as wild weeds, so they crush them. Then again, some farmers simply do not have a green thumb, meaning, they don't understand the tasks they've taken on. Then again, there are some cases where pastors genuinely do deal with wild weeds who have no desire to learn; they simply go from church to church looking for someone they can rule over. Either way, it is important to identify your own unique experience and determine what role you've played in the offense. By doing this, you examine your own fruit so that you can take from the experience what God wants you to take from it.

The garden that we plant ourselves in is important to God. As a matter of fact, scientists believe that composition and location of soil impacts the taste of fruits and vegetables. This is why people will pay more to buy wine from Italy, for example. Most people don't buy Italian wine because it's from Italy; they buy it because to them, it simply tastes better than American wines. After all, wine is made from grapes. Let's apply this same concept to the ministries we involve ourselves in. Some people are sour because they've been planted in the wrong churches for far too long, never stopping to ask God what He wants them to do or where He wants them to go. Consider the location of the fig tree that Jesus cursed. It is possible that the tree was not planted in the ideal location. Maybe there was no water for miles and no one around to water it. Maybe the wind picked up the tree when it was but a seed and carried it to its location — a location that would not be beneficial for its survival. Again, where you are planted is important to God, after all, not every church has been established by God. Some are nothing more than theaters that people go to perform. This is why we must have a personal and intimate relationship with God so that we can know His voice from the voice of a stranger.

God gave us the five-fold ministry to ensure that we would be firmly rooted in Christ. He knew that the enemy was going to publish his own doctrines and use them to deceive the world. Ephesians 4:11-14 reads, "And he gave the apostles, the prophets, the evangelists, the shepherds and teachers, to equip the saints for the work of ministry, for building up the body of Christ, until we all attain to the unity of the faith and of the knowledge of the Son of God, to mature manhood, to the measure of the stature of the fullness of Christ, so that we may no longer be children, tossed to and fro by the waves and carried about by every wind of doctrine, by human cunning, by craftiness in deceitful schemes" (ESV).

The reality is —a lot of the church hurt that people endure today is the result of them being planted in the wrong soil. For this reason, when God comes looking for them to see what they've done with the talents He's given them, they are hard to be found. When they are found, they have no choice but to acknowledge that they've buried their talents out of fear. This is because they are not being properly taught to utilize those talents. Instead, they are like the fig tree that had no fruit to boast of when Jesus came.

Church Culture

In every religion, there are traditions better known as church cultures. In every denomination, there is another branch of church culture, and every church has established its own culture. Culture is our way of emotionally decorating our church homes; it is us putting our unique human fingerprint on our church experience.

Church culture can be good, but then again, it can be bad. The danger of church culture is that it establishes a set of rules that are separate from the will and Word of God. For example, in some religions, the people are not allowed to wear jewelry; they are taught that doing so is a sin. This belief comes from 1 Timothy 2:9-10 being taken out of context. Apostle Paul authored the First Epistle of Timothy and he was addressing Timothy, instructing him on how to delegate the ministry in Ephesus. If you'll notice, many of Paul's letters were addressed to specific churches regarding the cultures that were established in each church. Paul wasn't saying that it was a sin to wear jewelry; he was addressing a problem he'd heard about. The women were basically putting on a fashion show at church and, of course, this was a distraction. Paul, however, did not send this same letter to the churches at Corinth, Galatia, Rome, Philippi, Colossae or Thessalonica.

The problem is that we, the church, often take the rules established to address a behavior at one church and we try to apply it to all churches. Not only does this cause problems for the people at each local church, but it causes an epidemic of church hurt to arise both nationally and internationally. Imagine if Paul's letters to Corinth had been accidentally sent to Rome and his letters to Galatia had been accidentally sent to Thessalonica. The pastors at each church would have been trying to correct a problem that did not exist at that particular location. In other words, we can't use a broad-angled approach when addressing certain behaviors in any given church. We must always remember that every church has its own culture and every pastor knows (or should know) the common issues that plague his or her church.

In some churches, there is no door greeter; you simply come in and you may be intercepted by an usher while you're on your way to find a seat. Some churches do have door greeters, with some of them being not-so-friendly, while in other churches, the door greeters are super friendly. Again, this all boils down to leadership and church culture. It doesn't make one church better than the other. All too often, it's just a community's response to what is common in that community. For example, if you were to visit a church where the ushers aren't overly chipper, you may find that the church is often visited by overly pushy locals who don't like to be told where to sit. Of course, this doesn't justify the ushers' behavior, but it does explain it. The ushers may have noticed that whenever they were super nice, they were overlooked and mistreated, but when they took a firm stance, people started listening to them. If you were to visit such a church after having gotten used to going to a church where the greeters and ushers greet you with a hug and a smile, you'd experience what we commonly know as "culture shock." Dictionary.com defines "culture shock" this way: a state of bewilderment and distress experienced by an individual who is suddenly exposed to a new, strange, or foreign social and cultural environment.

We experience culture shock when we visit other countries, states, communities and churches. Howbeit, we often forget about culture when we visit new churches because we expect all churches to operate the same way. A good example is this: in some churches, you'll find that the first few pews are filled with a bunch of women wearing all white, but in other churches, the front pews are simply filled with male and female congregants. In some churches, it is culturally acceptable for the congregation to scream, "Preach" while the pastor is teaching, while in other congregations, such behavior is not tolerated. The point is: some church hurt is nothing but culture shock; it is derived from a negative response to a behavior that a particular body of believers deemed to be offensive or blasphemous.

Just like each church has a culture that's unique to it, every church, as a whole, has a certain level of maturity. A church's overall maturity can be measured by that church's response to foreign

Church Culture

cultures. For example, let's say that your pastor has been invited to preach at a conference three states away. It's a large international conference where several churches will come together to fellowship. Your pastor invites the entire church and more than fifty percent of the members show up. That's around sixty members who have come out to support their pastor.

When you head through the doors of the church, the first thing you notice is a vending machine, but no door greeters. A few feet away from the vending machine is an ATM machine and a few feet from the vending machine is a small coffee shop.

After getting yourself a bagel and a cup of coffee, you make your way into the huge sanctuary with your fellow church members alongside you. There are no ushers. Instead, there are people lining the aisles greeting you, but no one is showing you where to sit, so you find a section big enough to seat all sixty of you. A few minutes later, a rather energetic woman rushes down the aisle and makes her way over to you. "Where are you all supposed to be sitting?" she asks in a rushed tone. Everyone

19

around you starts looking at one another, shrugging their shoulders and expressing that they are not sure. "What's your name? ... your pastor's name, I mean? What church are you from?" You answer her quickly because of her rushed tone and suddenly, she takes off back down the aisle without saying a word. Two minutes later, she's rushing towards you again. "You're supposed to be seated over there," she says, pointing to a line-up of chairs on the right side of the church. Everyone gets up and makes their way to the designated seating.

Service starts and instead of the choir coming to the stand, you notice a bunch of mimes standing on the stage, preparing to perform. Thirty minutes later, the church's pastor is up teaching and he says something that really stirs your spirit. Without thinking about it, you scream, "Amen!" and to your horror, you notice that most of the people there have turned around in their seats and started staring at you. Embarrassed, you apologize and the preacher proceeds with his sermon.

An hour later, your pastor is finally called to the stage and in a show of support, you and the rest of your church's members stand, scream and began to applaud as your pastor makes his way to the stage. The other churches that are there look at you all as if you've just collectively committed one of the deadly sins. After your pastor's sermon, another pastor makes his way to the stage, but his church's members give a very faint applaud. What you are experiencing is not just a local church culture; you are experiencing community or regional church culture, and if you're not mature, you'll write their behavior off as offensive. If you better understand culture, on the other hand, you'll see it for what it is and learn from it.

If you're new to a church, the best thing to do is to not take offense anytime you experience something that is foreign to you. You may be experiencing a church culture that you are not yet familiar with, but as the seasons change, you will come to better understand the traditions of that local body. Then again, if it isn't church culture and the people are just plain rude or messy, the wise thing to do is look for another church. At the same time, it is error to go into a church and try to bring your former church's culture into that church. Every local church body must respond to the needs of the people in their community.

The goal here is to rule out or better understand what you have experienced; whether it was church hurt or cultural indifference. Once you can identify the root of your experience, you can better address it.

Hurt from the Door

Excited about the idea of embracing a new life, Jasmine rushed to a nearby church, wearing a short black skirt, a sleeveless blue top, six inch black stilettos and a smile that could brighten the day. It was all she had to wear. However, before church service could even start, Jasmine's smile had been replaced with a look of confusion. Why the sudden change of heart? Jasmine had just made her way down the aisle and found herself a seat. Having noticed a few disapproving glares, Jasmine found herself tugging at her near knee-length skirt. "She did not just wear that to church." The voice came just a few feet from Jasmine. The speaker had attempted to whisper, but she'd failed miserably at it.

Feeling ashamed, Jasmine grabbed her purse and her brand new bible. She looked towards the back door, waiting for the aisles to clear so she could make a clean exit. That's when she felt someone touching her. Jasmine turned to her right and immediately saw the face of a woman she later described as an angel in disguise. The woman's name was Mrs. Ivory Morgan. "New here?" Jasmine nodded her head. "Yes," she said. "This is my first time visiting." Mrs. Morgan slid one of her hands into her purse. She twisted and turned her purse as she felt around the bottom of it. A few seconds later, she withdrew her hand from her purse and in it, she held three large peppermints. She placed two of the peppermints in her lap and proceeded to wrestle with the other hand. She had trouble keeping her hands still long enough to open the candy, so she grinned sheepishly at Jasmine and said, "Can you open this for me?" Jasmine smiled. "Sure," she said, placing her bible back on her lap.

Jasmine opened the peppermint and handed it back to her friendly neighbor. "Thank you," said Mrs. Morgan. "Here. Have one." Jasmine smiled and reached for the peppermint, but before she could speak, Mrs. Morgan had some words of wisdom to share with her. She leaned closer to Jasmine as she finished off her peppermint. She then whispered, "I had sausages before I left the house this morning. I ate this peppermint so I could tell you ... don't pay them any attention. You came here for Jesus, not them. Stay. I like having you next to me." Jasmine smiled. This was the beginning of her life's journey. Three Sundays later, Jasmine joined the church and ten years later, she was the first lady.

Jasmine had a happy ending, but sadly enough, not everyone has this testimony. Jasmine was like the many first-time visitors who enter a church wearing garments that most church folks consider to be inappropriate. The problem is that people who mistreat others based on what they're wearing on the outside are oftentimes people who are messed up on the inside.

Jasmine was new to the faith. She wore what she had in her closet, after all, her clothes represented her old lifestyle. Nevertheless, as time went on, Jasmine's heart was transformed and eventually, her new wardrobe matched her new mindset. The problem she'd experienced with her first visit was: she'd come in contact with people who had no love in their hearts. However, God knew what Jasmine needed, so He ensured that a sweet older woman by the name of Mrs. Morgan was seated in the right place at the right time. Jasmine's bad experience had been supernaturally countered by a good experience.

As we discussed in the previous chapter, every church has a culture and each church's culture has been cultivated by its leader. Some churches don't experience a lot of growth and for this reason, new visitors who walk through the doors will find themselves receiving uncomfortable stares from curious church members. If you've been in church a long time, these stares won't bother you too much because you'll understand that it's just culture in some churches. However, these stares can be downright intimidating and scary to a new convert. At the same time, in Jasmine's case, the stares weren't just coming from curious souls looking to get a glimpse of the new face; they were coming from judgmental believers as well. This is why we have to be mindful of our behavior towards others, especially new visitors.

Another similar story was submitted to me by a young woman named Aprah. Here's her story: One Sunday morning, I decided to go to Sunday school with both of my aunts. You see, my aunts were really into going to church and Sunday school. So, I asked if I could ride with them, and they had no problem with it at all. I believe I was in the tenth grade at this time, so I didn't really know any better. I didn't know how I should dress for church at the time, because I had been taught that it was a good thing to show your figure and shoulders. Since it was just Sunday school, I wore ripped jeans and a high-low tank top with crossed straps. The shirt was showing my shoulders and some of my back, but I honestly didn't look at it in a bad way. I was naive at the time; to me, that outfit was appropriate, specifically because of what I grew up around.

My aunt hadn't initially noticed how the back of my shirt was made until we were actually in the church and she'd sat behind me. She especially noticed it when I had to stand up and read out of the Sunday school book a few times. I believe one of the men in the church noticed too, and that was really what offended her. So, after Sunday school ended, both of my aunts and I got in the truck to leave, and then that's when my younger aunt went off on me. She said, " Why would you come to church with that outfit on?! You look like a hot and fast woman off the street." She was just constantly downing me and making me feel so guilty. My older aunt felt sorry for me and had to calm her down. My heart was broken, and I felt ashamed of myself; I felt disgraced. I even beat myself up, but the whole time, I also thought to myself that if she had just said what she'd said in a gentler way, I wouldn't have dealt with all of that pain and shame. She made me feel like a whore. Sadly, so many people go through that. When a person from church ridicules and overly criticizes someone over an honest mistake, that can lead people to not want to even go to church. It can lead to them being emotionally bruised. That's how I felt.

Aprah

Aprah's story is one that many women can relate to. I believe that we (the church) can get so caught up in being around saved people that anytime we come in contact with someone who isn't saved or someone who is a new convert, we chase them away with our words and our ways. Aprah's aunts were so worried about their own reputations that they forgot about her soul. She was a babe in Christ and as such, she needed to be welcomed, loved on and made to feel like a part of the family. Correction comes later when the believer has matured.

Matthew 19:13-15 reads, "Then were there brought unto him little children, that he should put his hands on them, and pray: and the disciples rebuked them. But Jesus said, Suffer little children, and forbid them not, to come unto me: for of such is the kingdom of heaven. And he laid his hands on them, and departed thence." Jasmine and Aprah were representatives of "little children." They were babes in Christ who simply wanted to draw closer to Jesus, but they were rebuked because of what they were wearing. This is a big mistake for any believer to make. Keeping God's children away from Him comes with some serious consequences. Luke 17:1-2 says, "Then said he unto the disciples, it is impossible but that offences will come: but woe unto him, through whom they come! It were better for him that a millstone were hanged about his neck, and he cast into the sea, than that he should offend one of these little ones."

We have to remember that every person we come in

contact with, whether they be in church or in the world, is in a certain place mentally, spiritually and emotionally. When we forget to demonstrate the love of God, we puff ourselves up and take on the same attitude that the Pharisee had in the book of Luke.

Luke 18:9-14 reads, "And he spake this parable unto certain which trusted in themselves that they were righteous, and despised others: Two men went up into the temple to pray; the one a Pharisee, and the other a publican. The Pharisee stood and prayed thus with himself, God, I thank thee, that I am not as other men are, extortioners, unjust, adulterers, or even as this publican. I fast twice in the week, I give tithes of all that I possess. And the publican, standing afar off, would not lift up so much as his eyes unto heaven, but smote upon his breast, saying, God be merciful to me a sinner. I tell you, this man went down to his house justified rather than the other: for every one that exalteth himself shall be abased; and he that humbleth himself shall be exalted."

When a new believer comes to Christ, the bible tells

us that even the angels in heaven rejoice. Luke 15:10 says it this way, "Likewise, I say unto you, there is joy in the presence of the angels of God over one sinner that repenteth." So, what does this mean for us: the believer? It means that we'd better deal with our own personal issues and be mindful of how we treat others, especially unbelievers who are desiring a relationship with God. It is unwise to allow church culture to overrule the love of God in your heart.

Did You Check the Fruit?

Every fruit tree starts off as a seed. It first springs from the ground looking like a simple plant, and eventually, if properly positioned and cared for, it will reach its full height. That's when the fruit will begin to bloom. After the tree has reached its full height, the fruit still has to go through the various stages of development. Once the fruit reaches its full size, it must go from being a bitter fruit to being a sweet-tasting fruit.

Most farmers can tell what stages their fruit trees are in by simply looking at them. Most farmers can tell you that not all red apples, for example, are ready to be eaten. They may look ready, but they aren't. Once the fruit is ready, it can be picked, but even after picking it, it needs to be washed off, especially if it fell to the ground.

There are many diseases that affect fruits. One such disease is called Apple Green Crinkle Disease and of course, it only attacks apples. Symptoms that an

apple tree is infected with Apple Green Crinkle disease are:
"Fruit - abnormal shape
Fruit - discoloration
Fruit - lesions: black or brown
Fruit - lesions: scab or pitting
Fruit - reduced size
Whole plant - dwarfing
When fruits on infected trees reach 1-2 cm in diameter, depressions begin to develop which eventually lead to malformation of the fruit. Brownish-red spots, which sometimes crack open, can develop on some cultivars. Malformed fruits are also small. In some cases, wart-like swellings may also develop on affected fruits, some of them covered by rough, brownish-red russeting. Vascular tissues below swellings or depressions are usually green-colored, hard and distorted. The symptoms resemble those caused by boron deficiency, although in the case of the latter, corky spots appear in the flesh of the apple (Kristensen, 1963; Smith, 1972; Drahorad, 1977; Németh, 1986)."
Reference: Plantwise Technical Factsheet/ plantwise.org)

Let's relate this information to the church you were hurt in. Did you check the fruit before you went in? Were there a lot of depressed, hard-hearted people and malformation (disorder)? Understand this: farmers can't just pick apples and sell them; they have to check them first. The same is true for us as believers. Matthew 7:16 (NIV) asks, "By their fruit you will recognize them. Do people pick grapes from thornbushes, or figs from thistles?"

Our problem is we hear the word "church" and totally disregard the fact that every church is run by imperfect people ministering to an imperfect congregation, meaning, it is a fruit-bearing institution that can be examined. Sure, we are imperfect, but even in our imperfect states, we must strive to honor God by loving each other, after all, it is impossible for us to love the Lord if we do not love each other. 1 John 4:20 reads, "If anyone says, 'I love God,' and hates his brother, he is a liar; for he who does not love his brother whom he has seen cannot love God whom he has not seen." In other words, the church must be pressing towards the mark of the higher calling; they shouldn't be unapologetically sinful or, in other words, rebellious and stiff-necked. The question remains: did you check the fruit? Why did you choose that particular church?

There are certain behaviors and spirits that operate very similar to viruses in local church bodies. They stop the development of the churches they affect by stopping the development of the people who attend those churches. They cause dwarfing: a local body's inability to grow beyond a certain point. Just like we have to address whatever it is that attacks our physical bodies, we must address the people and spirits that come to attack our church bodies. When certain personalities are allowed to serve in a church, those personalities will spread their love or their venom, depending on whatever it is they are full of. The same is true for uncorrected members who are not serving. There are some people who take the stage while seated in the pews. They tend to be loud, opinionated and overly determined to be heard and seen. These personalities can release a spirit of rebellion in any local body and start a string of disorderly behavior that, if not corrected, could destroy the church body that it is affecting.

Did You Check the Fruit?

Madeline wanted to find a church near her home, so one day, she conducted a few internet searches to find one. There were three in her vicinity, with the closest one being less than two miles away. Madeline was thrilled. She decided to visit the church that was closest to her and two Sundays later, she'd joined the church.

Almost immediately after joining, Madeline found herself standing before her pastor, trying to defend herself. As it turned out, Madeline had told one of the members that the pastor asked her for a ride home that Wednesday night. While this was true, Shelly (the woman who'd reported Madeline) hadn't told the pastor the entire story.

It was Sunday morning and service hadn't started yet. Shelly sat next to Madeline and almost immediately, she introduced herself. After a brief discussion about the layout of the church, Shelly said to Madeline, "I sure hope pastor is on time today. I heard his car has been acting up." Madeline didn't think before she spoke. "Yes, I took him home Wednesday night — wait — not to my house. He lives in the same city as me so I volunteered to take

37

him home — both him and his wife." Shelly smiled. She'd gotten what she wanted to get from Madeline. "Well, it was so very nice meeting you and I hope to see you again soon," said Shelly. She suddenly stood to her feet. To Madeline's horror, Shelly moved towards the front of the church and sat directly on the front row. Later that evening, Madeline found herself defending what she'd said and explaining why she'd volunteered to give out that information.

A few Sundays later, Madeline was on the internet in search of a new church home again. Her pastor hadn't forgiven her and it was evident. Shelly, ashamed of what she'd done, had stopped speaking to her and Madeline suddenly felt like most of the people in the church were giving her the cold shoulder. What went wrong?

The problem was Madeline looked for a church that was close to her home, but not one that was close to her heart. Sometimes, people think from a religious standpoint, whereas, they focus more on being connected to a church versus being connected to the right church. Madeline didn't check the fruit of the church; she only checked to see how far it was from her distance-wise. This is one of the most common reasons for church hurt.

Matthew 7:16 tells us that we will know them by their fruit. Even though the scripture is referencing false prophets, it is still an effective guide for any one in search of a church home or somewhere to simply fellowship. How uncomfortable are you when you sit next to someone who clearly has a cold or, even worse, the flu? That's because you don't want to catch what they have and you understand that it is contagious. Why don't we understand that a sick local church body is contagious? And sometimes, you won't know that a body is sick until it affects you. In other words, you shouldn't just join a church just because it's the closest church to you. If you do this, you may find yourself linked up to a local body whose culture and fruit are poisonous to your destiny.

When buying bananas from the store, you likely consider how often you eat bananas, how long it'll be before you eat the bananas and whether the stage of maturity that the bananas are in will allow you to eat them within that specific window of time.

If you know you won't eat them for a few days, you'll likely buy green bananas or slightly green bananas because they are not mature yet; they aren't fully ripe. This means that you can sit them on the kitchen table and not worry about them getting rotten. The same is true with every local church body. Every church is at a certain stage of maturity and if you're not prayerful and observant, you'll find yourself in the midst of bitter (immature) people or rotten (entitled) folks.

When considering a church home, you must consider how long you plan to attend that church, whether you want to make it your permanent church home, and what stages of maturity that particular church body is in. If it's an immature church, it simply may not be ripe enough for you yet. If it's a rotten church, you may find yourself fighting off the effects of bitterness. However, if it's a mature church, you still have to remember that even when an apple tree is fully grown, the fruit still has to go through several stages before it's ready to be picked. In other words, don't try to pick your church home; let God pick it for you.

Serving Laban

Sandra served under her leader, Mrs. Doe, for six years. When the two women initially met, Sandra was a member over at another church — a church that Mrs. Doe had visited. When Mrs. Doe saw how loyal and helpful Sandra was, she wanted her for herself.

When service was over, Mrs. Doe stood in the aisle a few feet away from Sandra, waiting for her to finish speaking with a couple who'd stopped to hug and chat with her. Mrs. Doe purposely positioned herself to intercept Sandra, and when Sandra finished speaking with the couple, she made her way down the aisle, waving at a few people as she walked. Suddenly, her eyes met with Mrs. Doe's eyes and the two women exchanged grins. "That is a pretty dress you're wearing," said Mrs. Doe. Sandra smiled. "Thank you so very much. Your dress is pretty too," Sandra responded as she continued to make her way towards the door. Needless to say, Mrs. Doe walked closely behind Sandra, stopping her in the foyer. "You have an amazing anointing on your life," said Mrs. Doe. "That's why I can't stop looking at you. I see such a glow emanating from you. Are you married?" Sandra looked at the small-framed older woman standing in front of her. "No ma'am," she said. "I'm divorced." Mrs. Doe cut in. "Cause I see a husband for you. He's a tall, medium-framed gentleman — very handsome — and he has a very lucrative job." Sandra couldn't wait to hear more. She'd always felt overlooked whenever a prophetic word was released and she was always taking care of the needs of others. She felt, in that moment, that this was her time. After chatting a few more minutes, Sandra walked away with Mrs. Doe's business card in hand. Six years later, she was struggling to get away from Mrs. Doe. She had never been promoted; she'd only served as Mrs. Doe's assistant.

Sandra was a prayerful woman and she felt like her prayers had finally been answered. She'd gotten a new job offer three states away, which meant, she would not be able to serve under Mrs. Doe anymore. Of course, the news was upsetting to Mrs. Doe and she did everything she could think of to get

Serving Laban

Sandra to stay, including telling her that the enemy (Satan) was trying to lead her away so he could attack her. Nevertheless, Sandra was tired of Mrs. Doe's antics, after all, she'd seen Mrs. Doe pull a similar stunt with a few other congregants who'd attempted to leave her church. A few stayed out of fear, but the ones who left seemed to prosper almost immediately.

Mrs. Doe refused to accept Sandra's letter of resignation, forcing Sandra to quit without notice. Five weeks later, Sandra started her new job in Arizona, but her ordeal with Mrs. Doe was far from over. She'd soon learn the extent her former pastor was willing to go to get her back.

Sandra found a new church home and almost immediately, she felt the presence of God; this was a feeling she hadn't experienced in years. After visiting the church a couple of times, Sandra decided to join. She also signed up for ministry classes.

Sandra began to share fliers, news and updates from her new church to her Facebook page and Mrs.

Serving Laban

Doe saw them immediately. "Be careful, Sandra. Last night, I dreamed that an evil man was going to trick you into believing that he was a man of God. He was gonna try to be your pastor and then, he was gonna try to sleep with you. Today, I woke up and saw the fliers you'd shared and my heart leaped when I saw your new pastor's face. He's the same man I saw in my dream!" Sandra was disgusted. Mrs. Doe was obviously still monitoring her life and had taken the liberty of sending her a message through her Facebook account. Sandra decided not to respond, and three Sundays later, she found out that the ordeal still wasn't over.

"Can I see you in my office?" It was Sandra's new pastor and he didn't look so happy. Sandra agreed. Five minutes later, she found herself sitting in her pastor's office alongside the pastor, his wife and one of the church's elders. "I got a message today from a woman claiming that you go from church to church trying to sleep with the church's leaders. Now, I don't give in to heresy, but because this woman had taken the effort to write me a long letter and mail it to my house, I wanted to make sure that I heard from you." Sandra's heart leaped. Immediately, she

44

knew who'd sent the message. It was Mrs. Doe. "Hold on," said Sandra as she pulled her phone from her purse. I have something I want to show you." Sandra began to nervously use her fingers to scroll her phone and a minute later, she let out a giggle. "Huh," she laughed. "I'm not surprised. But look at this. She blocked me, but she didn't realize that the message would still show up in my inbox." Sandra handed her phone to the church's elder who, in turn, handed it to her pastor. Mr. Smith's posture seemed to change as he read the message Mrs. Doe had sent Sandra a few weeks earlier. He seemed to be a little relieved and not at all tense like he was when they'd first entered his office. "Is this your former pastor?" asked Mr. Smith inquisitively. "Yes," said Sandra. "I'm not the first person she's done this to. Anyone who tries to leave her church is blackballed by her; she does this when she cannot convince them to come back. As you can see, she told me that you were an evil man, even though she didn't know you. That's just how she is. She's the one who wrote you. She blocked me because she knew I'd contact her." Mr. Smith handed Sandra's phone back to her. He playfully spun from left to right in his chair and then, he looked at Mrs. Smith.

Serving Laban

"We've seen this behavior before," he said. "Isn't that right, sweetie?" Mrs. Smith nodded her head and smiled. "Yep," she said. "We're sorry that this is happening to you and I'm real glad that you held on to that conversation because we really like you. We were talking about you the other day — talking about how you seem perfect for our new evangelism class that we have coming up. We want to train you for it and then, let you train the others."

What happened to Sandra is not uncommon unfortunately. She'd found herself serving under a self-centered leader who loved what she brought to her ministry. Mrs. Doe was very similar to the ruthless bible character, Laban. The bible tells us that Jacob served Laban for seven years to get Rachel, Laban's younger daughter. Jacob was so smitten with Rachel that he was willing to operate as a slave for seven years just to have her hand in marriage. However, Laban was a trickster. He recognized that his house was blessed because of Jacob's presence, so he gave Leah to Jacob instead. The story reads, "And Laban said to him, 'Surely thou art my bone and my flesh.' And he abode with him the space of a month.

Serving Laban

And Laban said unto Jacob, 'Because thou art my brother, shouldest thou therefore serve me for nought? Tell me, what shall thy wages be?' And Laban had two daughters: the name of the elder was Leah, and the name of the younger was Rachel. Leah was tender eyed; but Rachel was beautiful and well favoured. And Jacob loved Rachel; and said, I will serve thee seven years for Rachel thy younger daughter. And Laban said, 'It is better that I give her to thee, than that I should give her to another man: abide with me.' And Jacob served seven years for Rachel; and they seemed unto him but a few days, for the love he had to her. And Jacob said unto Laban, Give me my wife, for my days are fulfilled, that I may go in unto her. And Laban gathered together all the men of the place, and made a feast. And it came to pass in the evening, that he took Leah his daughter, and brought her to him; and he went in unto her. And Laban gave unto his daughter Leah Zilpah his maid for an handmaid. And it came to pass, that in the morning, behold, it was Leah: and he said to Laban, 'What is this thou hast done unto me? Did not I serve with thee for Rachel? Wherefore then hast thou beguiled me?' And Laban said, 'It must not be so done in our country, to give the younger before the firstborn. Fulfil her week, and we will give thee this also for the service which thou shalt serve with me yet seven other years.' And Jacob did so, and fulfilled her week: and he gave him Rachel his daughter to wife also. And Laban gave to Rachel his daughter Bilhah his handmaid to be her maid. And he went in also unto Rachel, and he loved also Rachel more than Leah, and served with him yet seven other years" (Genesis 29:14-30).

The story goes on to tell us that even after marrying Rachel, Jacob continued to serve Laban, but one day, he decided that he was ready to take his wives and his children and move on. However, Laban's response was very similar to the responses that we hear from many leaders when their members try to resign. Genesis 30:25-36 reads, "And it came to pass, when Rachel had born Joseph, that Jacob said unto Laban, 'Send me away, that I may go unto mine own place, and to my country. Give me my wives and my children, for whom I have served thee, and let me go: for thou knowest my service which I have done thee.' And Laban said unto him, 'I pray thee, if I have found favour in thine eyes, tarry: for I have

Serving Laban

learned by experience that the LORD hath blessed me for thy sake.' And he said, 'Appoint me thy wages, and I will give it.' And he said unto him, 'Thou knowest how I have served thee, and how thy cattle was with me. For it was little which thou hadst before I came, and it is now increased unto a multitude; and the LORD hath blessed thee since my coming: and now when shall I provide for mine own house also?' And he said, 'What shall I give thee?' And Jacob said, 'Thou shalt not give me any thing: if thou wilt do this thing for me, I will again feed and keep thy flock: I will pass through all thy flock to day, removing from thence all the speckled and spotted cattle, and all the brown cattle among the sheep, and the spotted and speckled among the goats: and of such shall be my hire. So shall my righteousness answer for me in time to come, when it shall come for my hire before thy face: every one that is not speckled and spotted among the goats, and brown among the sheep, that shall be counted stolen with me.' And Laban said, 'Behold, I would it might be according to thy word. And he removed that day, the he goats that were ringstraked and spotted, and all the she goats that were speckled and spotted, and every one that had some white in it, and all the brown among the sheep, and gave them into the hand of his sons. And he set three days' journey betwixt himself and Jacob: and Jacob fed the rest of Laban's flocks."

Simply put, Laban had absolutely no intentions of ever releasing Jacob. He loved the benefits of having Jacob around. This is what many people in the church have suffered through. Many have reported serving under leaders who loved the benefits of having them so much so that they refused to release them, promote them or ordain them. These people have served under their leaders for years, even showing up to serve when they weren't feeling their best. Nevertheless, nothing they did was ever enough and eventually, they realized that they needed to move on. They were in a bad relationship, and just like most people who entertain unproductive romantic relationships, they soon came to their senses and realized they were entertaining dysfunctional relationships with their leaders. However, when they tried to leave their churches, they fell victim to distraught leaders who felt like they'd been

Serving Laban

dumped. If this has happened to you, please know that you are not alone.

What should you do if you are trying to leave your church, and you clearly see that your leader is doing everything in his or her power to stop you? What should you do if your leader has a reputation for trying to destroy the names and character of anyone who leaves his or her church? Below are five tips that should help you.

1. If at all possible, give him or her your resignation letter. This is a honorary move that not only shows maturity, but it allows the leader ample time to find someone to replace you.
2. In some rare cases, you won't be able to send a resignation letter — especially if; for example, a new time-sensitive opportunity has suddenly opened for you or you know that your leader has blackballed others who've attempted to leave his or her ministry in the past. In these rare cases, it is better to secure your new job and then, send in the resignation once your job is secure. Be sure that you do not give the leader your new city,

state or the name of your job if you know that they will attempt to destroy any opportunity that arises for you.
3. If you're looking for a new church home, don't be so vocal about it. Just find one and then, resign.
4. Watch your words carefully and keep all communications between you and that leader. If the leader calls or emails you anything that could be considered gossip, slander or illegal, do not bite the bait! Keep your words holy and keep them few. Sometimes, the enemy is simply looking to have something to accuse you with!
5. The best advice of them all is: leave that church the moment you realize your leader does not have his or her emotions under control. Why wait to find a new church home or a job to leave? Once you identify that the fruit of a leader is not of God and this fruit is consistent, you need to save yourself and your family — get out of that church and fast!

What do you do when your Laban of a leader decides to punish you for leaving his or her church?

Serving Laban

Below is a few wise tips to help you move forward with as little incident as possible.
1. Again, if at all possible, give a resignation letter. If your leader refuses to accept the letter, send it to his or her certified mail. This step isn't to protect you legally because your leader cannot sue you for leaving his or her church, but shows your good-faith attempt to leave your church in a respectable manner. Please note that in some situations, you won't be able to give a resignation letter. For example, if you know your leader to be highly emotional and violent, it is best to email them your resignation letter, or if you know that your leader will call; for example, a company that is looking to hire you, it is best to keep quiet. Sadly enough, this is the reality for some church-goers.
2. If your leader or former leader emails anything offensive to you, do not respond. Sometimes, people do this to get a response out of you and they will use that response to accuse you to other leaders.
3. Remain respectful. Regardless of what your leader or former leader says, do not behave

carnally. Remember, it is not your job to put them in their places.
4. If your former leader is spreading rumors about you, do not contact them immediately. Instead, pray about the situation and speak with your current leader. Please understand that some people spread rumors in an attempt to get the people they are mad at to respond directly to them. Keep your current leader abreast with everything so they'll know how to pray for you.
5. If the rumors become slanderous, meaning, they are affecting you in some way (especially financially), have an attorney draw up a cease and desist letter and send it to them. This is pretty much a threatening letter that tells the slanderer that if he or she continues to slander you, you will take him or her to court.
6. Move forward; look ahead. One of the worst mistakes you can make is to constantly keep reflecting on what your former leader did. Remember, you have to forgive properly to heal properly. Don't go checking their

Facebook pages or rereading old messages. Just move on and forgive them.
7. Close that door entirely. It is not uncommon for a person (leader or not) to spread rumors and slander. When this doesn't work, they'll reach back out to the person they were attacking and attempt to restart a relationship with that person. That door is closed for a reason; leave it closed. Please understand that people who've tried to destroy your name and character will often apologize and try to restart the relationships they destroyed with their mouths because they need an extension on their attacks; they need to find something else to accuse you of. If you reopen those doors, you will give them the opportunities that they are seeking.

In Sandra's story, she made many mistakes that likely caused some huge blessings to be delayed in her life.
1. She should have told her current leaders about Mrs. Doe's invitation to join her church. Remember this: God is a God of order. Anyone who catches you in church and tries

to lure you out of it was not sent to you by God. Of course, if God didn't send them, the enemy did.
2. She should not have considered Mrs. Doe's invitation to join her church. Had she told her leaders, they may have told her to call Mrs. Doe, but decline her invitation — or they may have told her not to call Mrs. Doe.
3. Sandra should not have wanted a husband or a prophetic word so badly that she allowed Mrs. Doe's false prophecy to lure her. Sometimes, deceptive and ungodly leaders use prophecies, false prophecies and words of knowledge to lure people. If someone gives you a prophetic word, thank them for their willingness to obey God, submit that word to your leader for testing, and remain prayerful about it. If it is from God, it will come to pass.
4. Lastly, Sandra shouldn't have left the church that God had her planted in. Think about marriage. Once you're married, you become open game for adulterers and adulteresses. If you give them your time and your ears, they will try to sow discord in your marriage. They will then pretend to be the perfect

spouse for you, and if you're not wise, you'll fall for this scam. They will especially come after you when your spouse and you are in a bad spot in your marriage or if you start to feel like your spouse does not appreciate, understand or love you. Nevertheless, regardless of what's going on in your marriage, you have to remain firmly faithful — so much so that you refuse to give such people your phone number, your time or an opportunity to sow their wicked seeds.

Like Jacob, Sandra was blessed to get away from the person she once served. However, like Jacob, she wasted many years creating a story that should have never been told. Don't do this to yourself. Laban is only an effective weapon when he has something that you want and you're willing to serve him to get it!

The Position of Offense

When a fighter is standing before his opponent, he must take a certain stance; this position is called defense. Google defines the word "defense" this way: the action of defending from or resisting attack. In other words, the fighter must defend himself because he's standing in front of a fighter. The other fight must take the same position, but eventually, one or both fighters will break their stance and begin to swing at one another. This is true in most styles of fighting. Offense, on the other hand, is defined by Merriam-Webster this way: the act of attacking. So, to sum it up, offense is the act of attacking, but defense is defending one's self from an attack. For example, a defendant in a court case is simply defending himself or herself against the accusations of the plaintiff or prosecutor.

There was a woman on the usher's board at a particular church who was very mean-spirited. She held the position of the president of the usher's board, even though she did not possess the

The Position of Offense

personality of an usher. She was often very rude to people. She would talk loud to people who asked her questions that she did not want to answer, even though the questions were questions that were commonly asked to ushers. Additionally, she also did not like small children, especially infants because of her inability to control them. She couldn't scare a baby into silence. Oftentimes, she would have to ask people to tighten up or scoot closer together so more people could fit on their pew, but if they did not move fast enough or at all, she would say things like, "Do you want me to move you?" Occasionally, someone would address her negative conduct as an usher; sometimes, pushing and name calling would take place. Of course, many people reported her to the pastor and deacons of that church, but nothing was done to correct her behavior. As a result, many of the church's members said they couldn't take her attitude anymore and they moved their memberships to other churches.

What happened in this story is the usher's behavior was offensive and this provoked people to become defensive. The usher took on the stance of a fighter and this caused many people to also position themselves for a fight. It goes without saying, people should never feel the need to defend themselves while in church. People come to church to open up themselves and receive a deposit from God. However, wherever the spirit of offense is, the people will begin to close themselves off in an attempt to guard themselves.

Of course, the usher was a huge problem and the leaders should have removed her from her position, but the biggest problem was the leaders' failure to address and respond to the cries of the people. Understand this: a leader is seen by his or her congregants as a father-figure and one of the attributes of a father is that he is a protector. When people don't feel protected by their leader, they leave.

A lot of people sign up for or accept positions that they simply are not graced for. When a person is in the wrong position, that person will work against the church that he or she is serving in. This, undoubtedly, is a set up from the enemy to close churches and give Christianity a bad name. Each leader is supposed to examine the fruit of the people who serve under him or her. When the fruit is rotten, it needs to be uprooted and sat down. Matthew 7:18-20 says it this way: "A good tree cannot bring forth evil fruit, neither can a corrupt tree bring forth good fruit. Every tree that bringeth not forth good fruit is hewn down, and cast into the fire. Wherefore by their fruits ye shall know them."

Another sister went to her pastor about a problem with another female member of the church. She wanted advice from the pastor as to how she should respond to the woman who was spreading lies about her to other members. The pastor told her not to worry about it; he said that nothing would come of the lies. The pastor later started publicly preaching the information he had received from the member in confidence. Needless to say, the sister felt betrayed and stopped going to that church.

Again, a pastor is like a parent to his or her congregants. If the members of the congregation feel exposed to attacks from other members, they'll simply get up and leave that particular church. Sadly enough, many people leave the church altogether. One of the biggest issues we see is that the men and women who are in a position to correct others are not protecting them from the wolves that come in to devour them. This is especially true when the wolves are willing to serve.

We must remember that each church is a local body of believers and every believer has a function. If a member is serving in any capacity, that member's behavior will be seen as a reflection of the church and the church's leader. That member is serving as an essential part of that church's body and as such, he or she has the ability to affect how that particular body functions. The Word tells us how to deal with certain members of our bodies when they are not functioning the way they are designed to function. Matthew 5:29 reads, "And if thy right eye offend thee, pluck it out, and cast it from thee: for it is profitable for thee that one of thy members should perish, and not that thy whole body should be cast into hell." Matthew 18:8 goes along to say, "Wherefore if thy hand or thy foot offend thee, cut them off, and cast them from thee: it is better for thee to enter into life halt or maimed, rather than having two hands or two feet to be cast into everlasting fire."

The Position of Offense

What does this mean to local church bodies? It's simple: it is better to be without a keyboardist than to have a keyboardist who hurts the rest of the body. It is better to not have an usher than it is to have a bitter usher who keeps striking against anyone who makes her do her job. It is better to not have a praise team than it is to have a bunch of folks who do more complaining than they do praising. Proverbs 17:1 sums it up beautifully. It says, "Better is a dry morsel and quietness with it than a house full of feasting with strife" (NASB).

Let's think of it this way: Every house has a foundation and when that foundation begins to shift, the house can sustain structural damage. Some of the signs of structural damage to a building are:
1. Doors begin to get stuck or they won't lock.
2. Windows start sticking or getting stuck.
3. Cracks in floor or unevenness in floor.
4. Cracks start appearing in the walls, especially around entrance points like doors and windows.
5. Gaps where doors and floors normally connect.

The Position of Offense

One of the important things to note is that this doesn't mean that the foundation of the house was not put in correctly. It simply means something has caused it to shift and when this happens, the entire building shifts. Structural damage can be expensive and it can be deadly. How does this relate to having people serving in the wrong positions within their local churches? The answer is obvious: the vision of the pastor can be godly, but the wrong people can cause his vision to shift. Instead of focusing on the community and doing the things that need to be done in and around the church, the pastor suddenly has to redirect his or her attention to problems that are arising within the church because of servants who don't understand the love behind serving. Offense comes in when the positioning is off somewhere. Sure, no church is perfect, but it has to be managed if it is to survive.

Top Five Reasons for Church Hurt

One of the worst parts of church hurt is knowing you've been betrayed. People don't ordinarily cry "church hurt" when the person who's hurt them is a person they aren't too acquainted with. The reality is: trust is an investment and anytime we make that investment, we want to see a positive return on that investment. Even though we understand that we are taking a gamble, it's hard for us to fathom being on the losing end when we deal with the church.

In counseling victims of church hurt, I've found that most of them felt more betrayed than they did hurt. They fluctuated between anger and hurt, with anger quickly becoming the more dominant emotion each time they recounted their stories. This is because most people who were allegedly hurt by the church were hurt by people they once respected or trusted.

There are many reasons that people in the church hurt one another, but the five main reasons that this

happens are:
1. Offense
2. Gossip/ Slander
3. Jealousy
4. Feelings of Betrayal
5. Love of Money

Offense

In every given offense, there is the offended and there is the offender. Now, the offender hasn't necessarily done something offensive, however, the offended party judged their behaviors or their words as cruel, insensitive and messy.

When dealing with other human beings, most of us understand what conversations to avoid. We even understand that body language is a language in and of itself, and as such, it sends a clear message to the people who can see us. For this reason, we smile at one another and we look for common ground to meet on. Needless to say, however, this doesn't always work. There's always going to be somebody somewhere who is easily offended, just like there's always going to be somebody who makes it a point to offend others. There are several reasons that God does not want us to be easily offended, with the main reason being: He hates discord. Ecclesiastes 7:21-22 gives us a clear visual of the heart of God in regards to offense. It reads, "Do not take to heart all the things that people say, lest you hear your servant cursing you. Your heart knows that many times you yourself have cursed others" (ESV).

Jealousy

Consider the story of David and Saul. 1 Samuel 16:14-23 tells the story of their meeting: "Now the Spirit of the LORD departed from Saul, and an evil spirit from the LORD terrorized him. Saul's servants then said to him, "Behold now, an evil spirit from God is terrorizing you. "Let our lord now command your servants who are before you. Let them seek a man who is a skillful player on the harp; and it shall come about when the evil spirit from God is on you, that he shall play the harp with his hand, and you will be well." So Saul said to his servants, "Provide for me now a man who can play well and bring him to me." Then one of the young men said, "Behold, I have seen a son of Jesse the Bethlehemite who is a skillful musician, a mighty man of valor, a warrior, one prudent in speech, and a handsome man; and the LORD is with him." So Saul sent messengers to Jesse and said, "Send me your son David who is with the flock." Jesse took a donkey loaded with bread and a jug of wine and a young goat, and sent them to Saul by David his son. Then David came to Saul and attended him; and Saul loved him greatly, and he became his armor bearer. Saul sent to Jesse, saying, "Let David now stand before me, for he has found favor in my sight." So it came about whenever the evil spirit from God came to Saul, David would take the harp and play it with his hand; and Saul would be refreshed and be well, and the evil spirit would depart from him" (NASB).

As you can see, Saul once loved David, but if you know the story, you know that Saul eventually sought to have David killed. 1 Samuel 18:6-16 tells us why Saul had a change of heart regarding David. It reads, "It happened as they were coming, when David returned from killing the Philistine, that the women came out of all the cities of Israel, singing and dancing, to meet King Saul, with tambourines, with joy and with musical instruments. The women sang as they played, and said, Saul has slain his thousands, and David his ten thousands.' Then Saul became very angry, for this saying displeased him; and he said, "They have ascribed to David ten thousands, but to me they have ascribed thousands. Now what more can he have but the kingdom?" Saul looked at David with suspicion from that day on.

Now it came about on the next day that an evil spirit from God came mightily upon Saul, and he raved in the midst of the house, while David was playing the harp with his hand, as usual; and a spear was in Saul's hand. Saul hurled the spear for he thought, "I will pin David to the wall." But David escaped from his presence twice.
Now Saul was afraid of David, for the LORD was with him but had departed from Saul. Therefore Saul removed him from his presence and appointed him as his commander of a thousand; and he went out and came in before the people. David was prospering in all his ways for the LORD was with him. When Saul saw that he was prospering greatly, he dreaded him. But all Israel and Judah loved David, and he went out and came in before them" (NASB).

The spirit of jealousy provoked Saul and caused him

to seek David's life. Proverbs 27:4 (NASB) says this about jealousy: "Wrath is cruel, anger is overwhelming, but who can stand before jealousy?" Song of Solomon 8:6 reads, "Set me as a seal upon thine heart, as a seal upon thine arm: for love is strong as death; jealousy is cruel as the grave: the coals thereof are coals of fire, which hath a most vehement flame."

When church hurt is the result of jealousy, it can be deep-rooted and traumatic because a person who's jealous of you is a person whose hatred of you is rooted deeply within themselves. This is why jealousy is as cruel as the grave. I've heard numerous stories where leaders have behaved like Saul towards the congregants or the leaders who once sat under them. However, it is unwise to sit under a person once you realize that that person is harboring hatred towards you, especially if that hatred is rooted in jealousy.

Feelings of Betrayal

One of the hardest things about dealing with other humans is trying to tip toe around all of the rules and beliefs that people set up around themselves.

For example, one woman may visit several churches, believing that each church is supposed to notice her absence whenever she does not come to church. She does not take the size of the church into consideration, nor does she care when a church is understaffed. That woman will spend quite a bit of her church life experiencing offense, but not because someone intentionally offended her. The issue is — her personal beliefs and guidelines made it almost impossible to not offend her. Even if a church passes her test and calls her when she does not show up, they will find that she has a lot more rules in store for them to abide by. They will soon find themselves being accused of wrongdoing because of her beliefs. She may call her experiences church hurt, but the truth is — she's the one hurting churches.

Feelings of betrayal can be justified, but then again, they can be the result of an individual's personal beliefs. For example, some people tend to come to church early every Sunday so that they can sit in the same seat. There's absolutely nothing wrong with this, but the problem arises once the person has sat in the same seat for several weeks or months. This leads them to believe that the seat is actually their own personal seat and everyone in the church should honor this. Before long, they stop showing up to church early because they believe their seat will be waiting for them. Needless to say, one day, they come to church and find someone else sitting in the seat that they consider to be theirs. This leads to them feeling offended and sometimes even disrespected. If they ask the person to move and the person refuses to move or the usher, for example, points them to another seat, they will find themselves feeling angry, betrayed and again, disrespected. Such a person may come to the pastor and voice his or her complaint, only to hear the pastor reminding them that there are no assigned seats. No person can just label a seat as his or her own seat, unless otherwise assigned by the pastor. Feeling betrayed, the woman may leave the church. Now, this isn't an issue of church hurt; it's an issue of pride and entitlement.

It goes without saying that there are some cases where a person feels betrayed and their feelings are justifiable. For example, let's say that a woman tells her pastor something in confidentiality, but the pastor shares that information with someone else. The woman who confided in her pastor has the right to feel betrayed; her feelings are not without merit. If that woman or anyone who's been hurt does not receive the healing needed to move forward, they will hurt others, after all, hurt people hurt people.

Love of Money

1 Timothy 6:10 reads, "For the love of money is the root of all evil: which while some coveted after, they have erred from the faith, and pierced themselves through with many sorrows."

Interestingly enough, the average believer remembers the first line of this scripture, but does not remember or consider the rest of it. It tells us that some people have coveted after money and this caused them to deviate from the faith. What is faith? Hebrews 11:1 defines it this way, "Now faith is the substance of things hoped for, the evidence of things not seen." Merriam-Webster defines "substance" as:

a.) essential nature: essence
b.) a fundamental or characteristic part or quality

So, what then is faith translated in modern terms? Faith is the essential or vital part of your prayers; it is what fuels your prayers. But that's not all. The second keyword is "evidence." What is evidence? Merriam-Webster defines the word "evidence" this way:

    1.) a: an outward sign: indication
       b: something that furnishes proof: testimony; specifically: something legally submitted to a tribunal to ascertain the truth of a matter
    2.) one who bears witness

So then, faith is also an indication of answered prayers, even before the answer manifests in the natural. It is something that bears fruit, and the best part is — it is one who bears witness or, better yet, stands in the gap for you. John 18:37 reads, "Then Pilate said to him, "So you are a king?" Jesus answered, "You say that I am a king. For this purpose I was born and for this purpose I have come into the world—to bear witness to the truth. Everyone who is of the truth listens to my voice" (ESV).

If a person has deviated from the faith, that person

has denied himself or herself the blessings that come with faith. It goes without saying that this leads to frustration, intimidation, and manipulation. This is how they have pierced themselves with many sorrows. It goes without saying that people who cause themselves many sorrows bring sorrow into the lives of others and this includes people in leadership. If a leader does not possess the faith that he or she preaches about, that leader will end up hurting more people than he or she is helping. That's because when people are unable to get fruit from God, they try to pluck it out of the hands of anyone who does receive it. In other words, the weight of expectation that such a leader would place on his or her congregation would be too much for them to bear.

There are many more undocumented reasons for church hurt, but the core of them all is self. Selfish ambition, self-pity, low self-esteem, self-exaltation, and every form of selfishness is self-worship, also known as idolatry. When a person makes an idol out of himself or herself, that person will expect to receive everything that he or she associates with being a god. This is why we must humble ourselves and we must do this daily. When we do not embrace humility, we set ourselves up to hurt others and eventually be humiliated. When we tear down the altar of self, we soon come to understand the heartbeat of love and the compassion that flows from it.

Gossip in the Church

Most of us have been the victims of salacious gossip and we've all felt the need to defend ourselves at some point. Church gossip can be very traumatic and damaging, not only to the character of a person, but also, to the name and reputation of that person. To understand how to overcome gossip, especially gossip from church members and leadership, you must first understand the root of gossip.

Your name is the torch you'll pass on to your children, grandchildren and so on. It is what distinguishes your family from other families; it is your legacy. Your first name is what distinguishes you from your family. Because names are important to God, they are also what the enemy targets. Ecclesiastes 7:1 reads: "A good name is better than precious ointment; and the day of death than the day of one's birth."
Why does this scripture say the day of death is better than one's birth? Well, it has everything to do with your name. When you're born, your identity is

wrapped up in your parents' identities. You are your parents' new baby; that's it and that's all. Your surname identified whose child you were, and you weren't expected to do anything but to be a baby. At that time, you hadn't made your mark on society; you were just another cute baby. However, as you grew older, your identity began to develop and your first name started to take on a life of its own. Slowly but surely, you began to put your own unique fingerprint on society. The day you leave this earth is the day that your fingerprints should be covering every assignment God has given you. On that day, your identity will be completely separate from that of your parents' identity. That's why the day of death is better than the day of birth. You were born a sinner, but once you got saved and gave your life to Christ, you were born again.

"Surname, also called family name, or last name, name added to a "given" name, in many cases, inherited and held in common by members of a family. Originally, many surnames identified a person by his connection with another person, usually his father (Johnson, MacDonald); others gave his residence (Orleans, York, Atwood [i.e.,

living at the woods]) or occupation (Weaver, Hooper, Taylor). A surname could also be descriptive of a person's appearance (Little, Red) or his exploits (Armstrong)."
(Reference: Encyclopedia Britannica)

A few scriptures that address names and surnames include the following:
Genesis 12:2 reads: "I will make you into a great nation, and I will bless you; I will make your name great, and you will be a blessing."
Genesis 17:5 reads: "No longer will you be called Abram; your name will be Abraham, for I have made you a father of many nations."
2 Samuel 7:9 reads: "I have been with you wherever you have gone, and I have cut off all your enemies from before you. Now I will make your name great, like the names of the greatest men on earth.
Revelation 20:15 reads: "I will make you into a great nation, and I will bless you; I will make your name great, and you will be a blessing."

What do these scriptures tell us? They tell us that names are very important to God; they not only identify your natural father, but they help God to identify where you are. Of course, since our names are of utmost importance to God, the enemy has taken an interest in them too and this is why he throws gossip in the mix.

Gossip is designed by the enemy to destroy a person's name and reputation, since our names aren't just how we are identified by others, but our names will be passed down to our children and our children's children. If the enemy can destroy your name, he can destroy your legacy. Think of it this way: if a man was convicted of murder, his children would be identified by society as the sons and daughters of a murderer. Their names and personal identities would be overshadowed by their father's crime. To get rid of the stigma attached to their names, they would need to move to a place where no one knew them and try to start over. Howbeit, it would only be a matter of time before their father's legacy found them. The good news is that they can re-brand their father's name; the bad news is that it will take some time to do so.

Gossips feed on the attention they get from the people they are gossiping to. Gossip is, in a sense, their offering to others. Without it, they feel empty-handed and incomplete. Without it, they are forced to see their own failures, so gossip is pretty much like drugs and alcohol. It helps gossips to temporarily escape their own realities by focusing on the failures and hurts of others. Nevertheless, just like an alcoholic or a drug addict, gossips have to eventually sober up to their own realities. When their realities start overwhelming them, they go out and hunt for more gossip.

Gossips build relationships with two types of people: people they want to gossip to and people they want to gossip about. Howbeit, because they are gossips, the people they want to gossip to often find themselves being gossiped about as well. It's pretty much like the saying: there is no honor among thieves. In other words, a thief cannot trust another thief, even if they are working together. Also consider Proverbs 21:10, which reads, "The soul of the wicked desireth evil: his neighbour findeth no favour in his eyes." This means that a wicked person does not favor anyone; your proximity to an evil soul won't give you favor with that person. All the same, being close friends with a gossip won't get you any preferential treatment with that gossip. Eventually, you will find yourself wishing you'd stayed far, far away from them.

Gossips are like coal miners; they dig, cut and blast others in an attempt to find what they consider valuable. And just like coal miners, they often find themselves trapped or buried under their own words. They find value in the pain of others because they themselves are hurting. Remember: hurt people hurt people.

What should you do if you are the butt of church gossip? First and foremost, remind yourself that the gossip is a hurting person. Next, ask yourself this question: what role do I play in what I'm going through? The reason this is important is if you do not take accountability for your own mistakes, you won't learn from them. Maybe you gossiped with the gossip. Maybe you let that person into your life, knowing that he or she was a gossip. Maybe, you didn't know the person was a gossip, but once God revealed the truth to you, you didn't separate yourself fast enough. Maybe, you shared too much of your personal business with that person. It is important for a person to identify his or her own mistakes before a matter can be effectively resolved.

Next, remember, there is order in all things. You should never confront a gossip when you are angry or still in shock. Most gossips aren't just gossips; they are compulsive liars. Most will lie when confronted and if they sense that you do not believe their lies or if they can't lie themselves out of something, they will become defensive. Instead, the proper way to confront a gossip is outlined for us in Galatians 6:1, which reads, "Brethren, even if anyone is caught in any trespass, you who are spiritual, restore such a one in a spirit of gentleness; each one looking to yourself, so that you too will not be tempted" (NASB). Of course, if you're not spiritual — if you are too carnal or don't know how to be spiritual about the matter, the best thing is to speak to the church's leader first.

How do you restore a person? You approach that person in love and humility. You do this in private so that the person does not feel like he or she is being attacked or ganged-up on. However, before confronting someone about church gossip, please

Gossip in the Church

note that it is always wise to speak with the church's leader first; that way, if there is any backlash from the talk, the church's leader will be fully aware of the situation. Tell the leader what's going on and let the leader know that you plan to lovingly confront Sister Doe. If your leader prefers that you do so in an office setting with him or her in the meeting, follow the leader's instructions. Understand this: the leader may know that person better than you do, so that's why it is wise for you to adhere to wise counsel.

When confronting Sister Doe, you should say something like, "Hey, Sister Doe. Your hair looks really pretty today. Can I speak with you alone for a minute?" When Sister Doe agrees to the private meeting, you can say something to the effect of, "I love you and I respect you, and that's why I wanted to see you in private. There is a rumor out about me and a few people have told me that you've said this and that about me. I'm not looking to see what's true or not true; I'm not here to confront you about it. I just wanted to bring your attention to it and I wanted to ask you if there's anything I can do for you. Have I done something to offend you? If so, please let me know what it is so I can give you the apology that you deserve. If you need to talk with me about something or if you're going through something, I just want to let you know that I'm here for you." Now, understand this: you've just done something that the Bible calls "reaping hot coals" over another person's head. What this means is: you've just buried the coal miner. Proverbs 25:21-22 says it this way, "If your enemy is hungry, give him food to eat; and if he is thirsty, give him water to drink; for you will heap burning coals on his head, and the Lord will reward you."

Sister Doe is going to feel ashamed and, at the same time, she will feel betrayed by whomever it is that told you what she said. This means that in that moment, she is going to deal with a host of emotions and of course, she is going to try to lie her way out of it. She may become defensive or she may become wordy; either way, your goal isn't to accuse her. Your goal is to restore her. Once she's done talking, regardless of what she says, let her know that you love her and you're there for her if she needs you.

Because you approached her in love, you caused her words to backfire because gossips expect confrontation. However, they prepare themselves for angry confrontations and not loving ones. This means that Sister Doe will not be prepared for your response. In some cases, the gossip may overreact, get loud and get confrontational, but if this happens, the best thing to do is walk away. Don't say things like, "Keep my name out of your mouth" or "I said what I had to say." Such words will only aggravate the situation. If you spoke with Sister Doe privately, the next thing to do is bring the leader up-to-speed with the situation so that he or she can take it from there. This is proper protocol and it stops the gossip from destroying the church.

Now, what if the gossip is the leader? What should you do? It's simple: you follow the same steps. If the leader has a Bishop or Apostle, speak with them first. You do this to protect yourself from further damage. Follow the Bishop or Apostle's instructions and always make sure you are prayerful before any meeting you have with the offender or alleged offender. If nothing is done to rectify the matter or if your leader starts attacking you from the pulpit, it is best to pray and find another church. The reality is: you can't force people to like or respect you; sometimes, you just have to dust off your feet and move on to prevent further damage. Matthew 10:14 says it this way, "And if anyone will not receive you or listen to your words, shake off the dust from your feet when you leave that house or town" (ESV). Additionally, Psalm 34:14 says, "Turn away from evil and do good; seek peace and pursue it" (ESV). In other words, depart from any place where you don't have peace.

Slandered by a Former Church

Gossip and slander are similar, but they are not the same. A gossiper gossips about any and everyone, but a person who slanders others is more targeted in his or her attack. A slanderer is intentionally trying to stop or hinder another person's progress. Slanderers are focused primarily on the people they want to harm. For this reason, most people who have been slandered were not slandered by the people at their current church homes; they were slandered by people from their former church homes.

Gossips don't always use slander with the intent of harming others. They simply get high listening to and talking about others, regardless of who they are. Again, this helps to distract them from what's going on (or not going on) in their own personal, defective lives. This is why they are called busy bodies; they are always busy prying into other folks' lives. However, slanderers intentionally seek to harm whomever it is that they are gossiping about.

For this reason, in the United States, we can actually sue a slanderer for defamation of character.

The following information was taken from injury.findlaw.com: Defamation laws protect the reputations of individuals and other entities (such as businesses) from untrue and damaging statements. Libel refers to statements that can be seen (typically written and published), while slander occurs when a defamatory statement is spoken or otherwise audible (such as a radio broadcast). To prove either type of defamation, plaintiffs must prove the following four elements:
1. First, the plaintiff must prove that the defendant made a false and defamatory statement concerning the plaintiff.
2. Second, the plaintiff must prove that the defendant made an unprivileged publication to a third party.
3. Third, the plaintiff must prove that the publisher acted at least, negligently in publishing the communication.
4. Fourth, in some cases, the plaintiff must prove special damages.

(Reference: findlaw.com/ Elements of Libel and

Slander)

Slander can be hard to prove when it's not published, meaning, the slanderer has not written or recorded whatever lies he or she is telling about you. And since slander is hard to prove, it's hard to address. The truth is: most people assume that someone from their former church is slandering their names or their character when they find themselves not being able to explain a series of misfortunes in their lives. For example, let's say that Mr. and Mrs. Doe are members at the same church, but the couple is going through a divorce. Mrs. Doe decides to leave her church home to find another church because she does not want to run into Mr. Doe. At her new church home, Mrs. Doe notices that the people aren't overly friendly like they were at her former church home. Instead, everyone seems relatively distant and the church is full of cliques.

One day, Mrs. Doe tries to sit next to three women who happen to be hurdling together and laughing about something. When she makes her way to the seat, the woman seated directly next to the seat says, "I'm sorry. This seat is already taken." Feeling rejected, Mrs. Doe goes and finds herself another seat. The woman seated next to her suddenly gets up and moves over a seat. At this point, Mrs. Doe feels rejected and targeted. Without warning, she looks up and sees a guy that she recognizes and he happens to be one of Mr. Doe's co-workers. Church hasn't started yet and Mrs. Doe has already developed a theory in her heart. She believes that Mr. Doe's co-worker told him that she started attending the same church he attends. She also believes that Mr. Doe slandered her name to the guy and now, Mr. Doe's co-worker is spreading rumors about her. This is a case or assumed slander, not necessarily actual slander. This is why slander is so hard to prove; sometimes, a series of coincidences will lead people to believe that their names are being slandered. In Mrs. Doe's story, the case may very well be that she's going to a church where the people aren't that friendly to outsiders. Sadly enough, there are many churches out there like that, especially in small towns or communities.

When dealing with church slander, you should never assume that someone is slandering your name if you do not have any evidence to prove your beliefs. With no evidence, you have nothing but an elaborate theory. However, if you do have evidence and you know for sure that someone is intentionally trying to destroy your character, the first thing you have to do is address yourself. You have to make sure that you are emotionally prepared to address the issue. All too often, we try to address gossip, slander and offense when we are upset and this only amplifies the problem. It is easy for a victim to look like the problem-maker if the victim is out of control emotionally.

Next, you need indisputable evidence that the alleged slanderer is attempting to slander your name. Heresy does not count; you need actual evidence. Someone simply telling you that another person is speaking reproachfully about you is not enough. Why not? Because the person may be a liar, a gossiper who's simply trying to pry, or a concerned party simply acting as an informant only. People who act as informants simply want to tell you what they've heard, but they won't be willing to help you any further than that — in most cases.

If you have indisputable evidence outside of heresy,

the next step is to approach that person's leader with the evidence. In the previous chapter, I recommended that you speak with the gossiper in private after, of course, you've cleared it with your leader, but when dealing with a slanderer, you have to use a different approach. Again, most gossipers aren't necessarily trying to destroy your reputation; they are like alcoholics: they simply have a problem with their tongues. Slanderers, on the other hand, have a problem with you. In some cases, people who intentionally try to destroy your name are trying to lure you to themselves. In other words, they want you to confront them because they don't know how to approach you. Should you approach a slanderer, you will often find that the person has a lot of anger, hatred, malice or jealousy in his or her heart towards you and that's why it's not a good idea to address such an individual privately. Instead, you need to speak with that person's superior, whether that superior be his pastor, bishop or apostle.

If the slander is coming from leadership, the best way to deal with it is to collect the evidence and hire an attorney to send a cease and desist letter, detailing your complaint and demanding that the behavior cease. Do not take them to court, as the bible instructs us not to take our brethren to court, but a cease and desist letter should be enough to let them know that their behaviors will not be tolerated. If the cease and desist letter does not work, you should speak with your local leaders and a few attorneys to see how the matter can be resolved.

Lastly, don't put so much faith in the effectiveness of a slanderer. All too often, I've witnessed people overreact to another person's attempts to put a blemish on their names. The worst part is — the slanderers didn't have the greatest of connections, meaning, they couldn't do much damage. The slanderer was simply trying to get his or her victim's attention; that's it and that's all. Maybe the slanderer was jealous of the person; this is not uncommon. Maybe the slanderer is reacting to some lies he or she has heard. Maybe the slanderer feels rejected or victimized by that person. Sometimes, people will do silly things to get attention. If you reward them with the attention they are begging for, you only hurt the matter further. Sometimes, the best approach is to simply ignore the person. Sometimes, people measure their success, not by what they accomplish, but by the names and the accomplishments of the people whose attention they've managed to get.

The Church Hurt Epidemic

According to Pew Research Center, the Christian population is on the decline in the United States, dropping nearly eight percent from 2007 to 2014. Even though we're still considered the largest religious group in the world, our numbers are decreasing astronomically. Many people are leaving the church and some are turning to other religions in an attempt to find themselves. Of course, there are many reasons for this faith decline and one of those reasons is an epidemic that most people don't want to talk about and that epidemic is church hurt.

As an African American growing up in the South, we were taught to keep people out of our family's personal affairs. Whatever happened in our house was to stay in our house, regardless of how big or small it was. Violating this rule could get you in a lot of trouble, not just with your parents, but with your family and community as a whole. I believe these rules are pretty much universal; they can be found in every racial arena. It's not just a Southern thing, after all, a large number of Northerners are descendants from the South and vice versa.

When many of our ancestors moved to the North, they took their rules with them, so what was once Southern culture is now a universal law of sorts. Additionally, these rules have spilled over into the church and this is why we don't like to talk about what goes on in the church. Every church body tries to manage its own dysfunction and every church body works hard to keep outsiders, including neighboring churches, out of their business. Howbeit, as most of us know, that rule did more harm than it did good. Families suffered in silence when help was readily available for them. The same is true in today's church.

If you openly speak about church hurt, you'll likely hear people directly or indirectly saying things like, "Build a bridge and get over it." That's the easy way to address such a complex issue. With leaders having such a small window of time to minister each week, I believe that many leaders try to rush people to the finish line without teaching them how to prepare for the race itself. Getting over church hurt is a lot easier said than done and if you've ever been hurt by a leader or a member of a church you were affiliated with, you know how hard it is to move forward. The reason is we tend to be unguarded when dealing with our church family because, let's face it, we all need someone we can trust. We need someone we can open our hearts to, tell our secrets to and lean on in times of trouble, and many people simply don't have strong, supportive family units that they can lean on. So where does one go to find support, love and comfort? Most people come to church.

When you are a new believer or new convert, you are excited about the idea of finally having a strong, loving Christian family that you can lean on, spend time with and talk to. You're like a kid who's walked into a toy store for the first time: everything looks so promising. Nevertheless, as time passes, you soon discover that the same folks or personalities you've been trying to get away from are seated next to you in the pews. Even worse, you eventually come to realize that your leaders are flawed. Sure, most people say that they don't expect their leaders to be perfect but, in truth, they do. Eventually, reality sets in and you realize that there are certain people you want to avoid, sitting a few feet away from you in the church. As you matured in the faith, you came to realize that you had to roll up your sleeves and try to make the best of your church home. That's the reality of church bodies. However, to come to this reality, you had to stay put, do a lot of praying, a few sit downs with the pastor and resolve within yourself that no church is perfect because the people who make up the church body are imperfect. Then again, there are some of you who were in a completely different reality. You were a part of a church body where you've been abused, persecuted, attacked, ridiculed, rejected, mocked or excommunicated. You stuck around for years, trying to wait for things to get better, but they only got worse. Eventually, you decided to cut ties with that church, but the pain still plagues you to this day. If this is true for you, please understand that you are not alone.

Somewhere, there's a woman wandering around her house. She hasn't been to church in years, even though she believes in God and serves Him to the best of her ability. She speaks of God, reads her Bible often and even evangelizes when the opportunity presents itself. She is not one of God's castaways. She is the victim of church hurt, a growing epidemic in church arena today. Because of her personal experiences at one or more local churches, she has opted to have church at home. When she takes to social media, she soon realizes that there are many believers out there who are just like her — people who have unofficially become virtual church members, visiting their favorite pastors' YouTube pages daily or weekly. And just like her, most of these people are the victims of church hurt.

First and foremost, let's address church hurt in general. Unfortunately, there is no traditional definition of church hurt, but this epidemic seems to be more commonplace in today's Christian church, especially in the generation we refer to as the millennials. Additionally, it is not limited to a particular denomination. A non-traditional definition of church hurt is: hurt, offense or trauma brought on by a body, sect, or group of believers. It is oftentimes a series of unwelcome events, often believed to be perpetrated by the leaders or supervisors of a particular body. Most people who allege that they have been mishandled by the church are truly referencing the leadership of the church they were hurt in. If the hurt or offense came through another member of a particular body of believers, most people could overlook the offense, but when it comes from leadership, it is often referenced as church hurt, and this is understandable. After all, no one wants to be led by someone they believe who does not like them. And this is oftentimes the complaint. It's not just the offense itself that the believer often uses to justify disconnecting from a certain body of believers. In most cases, people who allege they've been hurt by their leadership believe that their leaders' hearts and intentions regarding them were impure. Such a theory is not often developed through one unpleasant encounter with a leader; it is developed when a series of failed communications seem to plague the relationship between the leader and the member. And in the rare cases that one member is offended by another member, in most instances, the referenced church hurt was not established until the offended party went to the leader about the other party. When the leader did not take action or the leader didn't take the action the offended party believed the leader should have taken, the offense was intensified. In such cases, if the disgruntled member continued to attend the church in which he or she was offended in, every visit and every encounter in that church is logged in that member's heart as supporting evidence that backs up whatever theories they have developed within their hearts regarding their leaders' heart towards them. For example, if a man believes that his pastor does not like him, he will closely monitor the pastor's behavior towards him, as well as the pastor's behavior towards other members. From that point on, he will scrutinize the pastor's tone, body language, words and behaviors. In other words, if the offense is not addressed properly, it will escalate.

Church hurt isn't new. As a matter of fact, church hurt is responsible for the establishment of many religions and churches. For example, if I had a small town church in the early 1900s and one of the members didn't like the way I ran the church, he would likely confront me about it. If I didn't respond the way he wanted me to respond, he would probably go and open a church for himself up the street from my church. He would have slightly modified the doctrine that I taught, became more charismatic in his teaching style, appealed to a certain age group, and proceeded to start an entirely new church or religion. This means that his decision to open another church more than likely had nothing to do with the doctrine that I taught; it had everything to do with him being offended with me.

The World Christian Encyclopedia reports that in 2001, there were approximately 33,830 Christian denominations in the world. I am confident that a large majority of those religions are nothing but responses to church hurt. God knew that this would happen and that's why He told us how to handle offense. Matthew 5:23-24 reads, "Therefore if thou bring thy gift to the altar, and there rememberest that thy brother hath ought against thee; leave there thy gift before the altar, and go thy way; first be reconciled to thy brother, and then come and offer thy gift."

What God is telling us here is to address our offenses with one another, but because many in the church have failed to do this, we are seeing mass divisions among us. Church hurt isn't just a slight offense between two people. If it isn't addressed, it can divide a church, an entire denomination or an entire religion within itself.

Christians remained the largest religious group in the world in 2015, making up nearly a third (31%) of Earth's 7.3 billion people, according to a new Pew Research Center demographic analysis. But the report also shows that the number of Christians in what many consider the religion's heartland, the continent of Europe, is in decline. Pew Research also reported: The number of Christians around the world has nearly quadrupled in the last 100 years, from about 600 million in 1910 to more than 2 billion in 2010. But the world's overall population also has risen rapidly, from an estimated 1.8 billion in 1910 to 6.9 billion in 2010. As a result, Christians make up about the same portion of the world's population today (32%) as they did a century ago (35%).
(Reference: PewResearch.org)

With the growing number of people converting to

the Christian faith, it is safe to say that church hurt is going to continue to rise. Additionally, because of the record growth of the church, the pressure to keep up with that growth has led many leaders to ordain ministers who, quite frankly, are not called or equipped to head up the charge of ministry. This leads to a lot of ill-prepared and immature leaders who take out their frustrations on the people they are supposed to be ministering to.

Of course, it took me a while to learn to balance myself emotionally as a leader. Just like most leaders, I had to learn to minister to people who I simply could not relate to, and in order to do this, I had to enlist the help of the Lord. I learned to not take everything personal and to understand that hurt people hurt people. I also came to learn that not everyone who requests to be ministered to actually wants to be ministered to. Some people simply want to hear themselves talking out their problems, and once they're done talking, they've already decided what they want to do about the problems that are plaguing them. They simply wanted a listening ear. At the same time, some people want someone to vent their frustrations to.

They don't want to talk about their problems; they want to have someone to stand in place of the person who has hurt or offended them. For example, it's not uncommon for people to talk about something another person has done and begin to say to me what they want to say or wish they would have said to the other person. An immature minister may get offended with a person who does this and wound that person even more.

Church hurt has truly become an epidemic in today's church and if we don't address this issue at the root, we are going to continue to see divisions among us. Of course, this is what Satan wants. He wants to divide the church because he knows there is power in unity.

Genesis 11:6 reads, "And the LORD said, behold, the people is one, and they have all one language; and this they begin to do: and now nothing will be restrained from them, which they have imagined to do." What the Bible is referencing here is the people of God who were attempting to build the Tower of Babel. Because they were unified, the Bible tells us that God said out of His own mouth that absolutely nothing could be withheld from the people. For this reason, God confused the language of the people. In other words, in that hour, God created many different languages. This was one of the few times in the scriptures where we see God actually dividing His own people. This was because they were trying to illegally access heaven. Nowadays, we have trouble communicating with people who speak the same language. The issue isn't that our languages are necessarily confused; the issue is that we are confused. Many don't read the Bible for themselves and this opens the door for church hurt, after all, if you do not get to know God on an intimate level, how can you agree with anyone who teaches you about Him in a way that seems foreign to the God you believe Him to be? Unity is birthed in like-mindedness, but confusion is birthed in diversity. Amos 3:3 reads, "Can two walk together, except they be agreed?" Church hurt results when two people come out of agreement with one another. This means to cure the church as a whole, we need to all get into agreement with God; that way, there won't be divisions among us. Paul addressed division in the church of Corinth and he pinpointed the root of that offense. 1 Corinthians

11:188-22 reads, "For first of all, when ye come together in the church, I hear that there be divisions among you; and I partly believe it. For there must be also heresies among you, that they which are approved may be made manifest among you. When ye come together therefore into one place, this is not to eat the Lord's supper. For in eating every one taketh before other his own supper: and one is hungry, and another is drunken. What? Have ye not houses to eat and to drink in? Or despise ye the church of God, and shame them that have not? What shall I say to you? Shall I praise you in this? I praise you not."

What caused the divide within the church of Corinth? According to Paul, the problem was rooted in heresies. What is heresy? According to Merriam-Webster, heresy is: (a) dissent or deviation from a dominant theory, opinion, or practice, and (b) an opinion, doctrine, or practice contrary to the truth or to generally accepted beliefs or standards. In layman's terms, the church of Corinth was filled with opinionated people. Anytime a body of believers come together and do not agree about the doctrine or practices of a church, church hurt and offense are guaranteed to follow. This means that truthfully, church hurt can stem from the body just as it can stem from the leadership. It is not uncommon for a member of a church to attempt to correct their leader. This is disorderly and is oftentimes nothing but an attempt by that person to usurp the authority of their leader. When the leader rebukes the member and refuses to receive correction from that member, it goes without saying that the member will feel rejected and that rejection will be labeled as church hurt.

Again, somewhere, there's a lady roaming around her house who has not been to church in many, many years because of offense. As a leader in today's church, my instructions to that woman is: not all churches are the same and you shouldn't let anyone drive you into seclusion. Sometimes, the best thing to do is pray and seek God about sending you to another church, instead of becoming another silenced member of the body of Christ. We cannot fix what we do not address. We've got to learn to come to one another in love and do our best to make amends. We can discuss a lot of issues that take place in today's church, but if the root of the issue isn't addressed, we'll simply trim the issue, instead of uprooting it.

Understanding Each Body

Every (human) body is comprised of a single head. Without a head, the body cannot live, nor can it function. The same is true of a church body; there is a head or governing authority, and under each head, there are members. The direction that a body goes in is determined by the head, even though the members can communicate to the head regarding the direction they are heading in. Ultimately, however, the pastor must hear from God regarding the direction of the church he or she is pastoring. It is not natural for a human body to have two heads, just as it is not functional for two people to head up a single body of believers. Sure, to keep us humble, God allows the head of a church to have someone who is covering and heading up that leader, but a church with two pastors would be a church where confusion flourishes. With natural bodies and spiritual bodies, there has to be order, otherwise, there will be division. This is why it's important for you to know what member of the body you are in your church. I've witnessed people going into churches and trying to function as the head or governing authority. If this behavior is not corrected, division is inevitable and church hurt will soon follow.

As Christians, we are members of the body of Christ. Just as our natural bodies have limbs and organs, each person in the body of Christ has a specific function. When we individually discover what our functions are, our lives are made so much better because we won't assume roles that we are not equipped to have. Again, many people are not called, nor are they mature enough to head up a church, but because they don't know their functions in Christ, they will happily accept a role to pastor a church to the detriment of that church.

Just as we are all members of the body of Christ, every church is a body of believers, with each believer assuming a particular function. Some believers are active in the church, whereas, others are spectators. Either way, each person is a member of a certain body and that member is either functional or dysfunctional. It is important for us to determine our roles and whether we are functioning limbs and organs or malfunctioning. The truth of the matter is that people who function the least in church often expect the most from the church. This is largely due to each individual's view and understanding regarding the role of the church. Think of it this way. Your body is comprised of limbs. What if you expected your feet to carry the groceries? Your feet are functioning members of your body, but if you do not understand the role or function of your feet, you could easily lose your ability to walk. Because you understand the role of your feet, hands, eyes, nose, mouth, and ears, you know which limb or organ to utilize at any given time. The problem with most folks in the body of Christ is they don't understand their own roles or functions, nor do they understand the roles and the functions of the people who are connected to the body that they are a part of. What if your hands would not cooperate with your feet? What if your hands complained about having to carry everything around? What if your hands started protesting because, after complaining about having to carry everything around, it did not get the response, apology or change that it expected to receive from your feet? After all, your feet and your legs carry you, but if the hands could think on their own, they probably wouldn't understand or respect the role of your feet. God knew exactly what He was doing when He put all of our limbs and organs in one body and He gave that body one brain to operate by. If all of your limbs had minds of their own, you would probably experience what we are experiencing in the church today. Too many people who don't know, understand or respect the functions of their co-laborers.

One of the reasons church hurt is so prevalent is because people tend to treat churches like school districts. How so? The average believer did not pray and ask the Lord which church He wanted that believer to attend. Instead, most believers attend the churches closest to their homes or they attend the churches their families have been going to for years. This means that the average believer goes to church expecting to receive, but never expecting to function. One of the quickest ways to offend a malfunctioning member of a specific body is to tell that member to function. It's very similar to getting someone to exercise when that person is not accustomed to exercising. When we exercise, we use the muscles in our bodies, but if a person does not exercise, that person's muscles are weak. If pushed to exercise, that person would initially experience soreness. Nevertheless, any fitness instructor would tell you that even if you are sore, you must keep exercising and this, of course, can be very painful. The same is true when dealing with the body of Christ. Some members simply don't function much in the body, so when those members are pushed by the heads of their churches to finally start functioning, they will experience some discomfort. The ones who understand that the push is for their good and the good of the body as a whole will keep functioning, but the ones who are adamant about not changing will become sore and likely disconnect themselves from their body of believers. Many will go out and look for another body of believers to malfunction in, while others will stop going to church altogether. How we respond to being challenged and pushed often has nothing to do with the leadership of a church; it has everything to do with our expectations of the church.

There is a rare condition called Polymelia that can help us better understand what is taking place in

Understanding Each Body

the body of Christ. Wikipedia defines Polymelia this way: Polymelia (from Greek πολυ- = "many" plus μέλος (plural μέλεα) = "limb") also known as hydra syndrome is a birth defect involving limbs (a type of dysmelia), in which the affected individual has more than the usual number of limbs.
(Reference: Wikipedia.org/ Polymelia).

Simply put, Polymelia is being born with too many limbs; for example, in 2014, a Pakistani boy was born with three arms. The crazy part about this condition is that the extra limb is often misplaced and does not function. This normally happens when the remains of an underdeveloped twin gets attached to the other (developing) twin. As a result, the non-functioning member eventually has to be surgically removed. This is very similar to what happens when a believer tries to function in the wrong church body. So, for example, if you connect to the wrong church, you may become a non-functioning member, meaning, you are like a third arm or an extra nose. However, if you're like a lot of believers, you will feel the need to function and this often leads to contention when someone is functioning in a role that another believer believes

Understanding Each Body

he or she should be functioning in.

Many churches suffer from what can best be described as Spiritual Polymelia, whereas too many members are trying to function in one or more roles, or trying to function in roles that they are not designed for. This means that we have a lot of people who simply do not understand who they are in Christ Jesus and this leads to a religious attitude towards God, church and relationships. What is a religious attitude? It is one of performance and not love. It is centered around self and not the body of Christ as a whole.

What is your role in the church you are attending? Or if you're not connected to any body of believers, what was your role and why did you stop functioning in it? I am in no way implying that you are at fault because I don't know your specific situation, but it is important for you to address yourself so that you can start functioning the way God designed you to function. After all, as a member of the body of Christ, you are needed. Even more, you are needed in the specific body of believers that God has assigned you to.

Again, I believe that if every believer took the time out to inquire about their identities and roles in Christ Jesus, church hurt would not be the epidemic it is today. It would be more contained or quarantined to specific religions, but it would not be found in the true body of Christ. Church hurt is the result of malfunctioning heads and members; we have to accept this if we are going to get past it and finally come together once more in unity. That way, God can say of us what He said about the people who decided to build the tower of Babel. He would say, "Behold, the people is one, and they have all one language; and this they begin to do: and now nothing will be restrained from them, which they have imagined to do." What I love about this statement is the fact that the word "is" is singular, even though the word "people" is plural. In the English language, we use "are" instead of "is" when referencing a singular subject or noun. So, we would read the sentence this way, "Behold, the people are one, and they have all one language..." God used the word "is" to represent complete unity. He acknowledged them as one body, one person. Of course, Satan knows the power of unity and that's why he attacks each body of believers that he can gain access to. He ushers in heresies through opinionated believers who hate to submit to any and every form of authority. If these believers are not addressed, their rebellious natures will spread throughout the church like a virus and before long, that specific body of believers will dismember.

If you don't know your function, you will link up to a body that does not understand how to utilize you. They will have you functioning in the wrong role or functioning in the right role the wrong way. Nevertheless, if you know your function, it will be easy for you to walk inside a church and determine if that specific body is the one God has assigned you to function in.

Common Reasons for Church Hurt

As a leader, I've heard countless stories from people stating they've been mishandled, disrespected, mocked and even excommunicated from their churches. Of course, each person believed that his or her leader was at fault, and I'm sure if I'd spoken with the leader, he or she would have blamed the former member. As a Bishop, my role is oftentimes to simply listen because, again, some people hear themselves talking about the matter out loud, and this helps them to better see their own role in the offense. In some cases, however, I can clearly see the leader's error and there's no getting around it. It is oftentimes difficult to determine who was at fault, after all, both parties have their own perspective, and in most cases, both parties see themselves as the victim. Needless to say, I cannot correct a leader who is not in my jurisdiction or someone I do not know. In a situation like this, my goal is to help the member to move past the offense, heal from it and learn from it.

Who was at fault in your church hurt story? Sometimes, the answer can be found when you view the incident objectively. What could you have done to prevent the incident or incidents from occurring? What fault would you say that you have in the offense? In your opinion, what would have been a satisfactory resolution to the matter? What function did you have? Compare that with the function you wanted to have.

Below are some common reasons for church hurt. First, you'll find ten common infractions that leaders have reportedly committed, and after that, you'll find ten common infractions that members and non-members commit. Please note that when I reference "leaders," I'm not just talking about the pastor or the deacons; I'm also referencing the ushers and any member who comes in contact with a non-believer or non-leader.

When the Leader is at Fault

When the shepherd wounds the sheep, the wounds can often be pretty deep. Below are some common mistakes that leaders make:

(1). Favoring Members: In every thing, there is a

hierarchy. Most of us don't want to admit this, but it's true. So everywhere you go, you will fall in a certain order with every individual you come in contact with. This doesn't mean that you are not important; what it means is that it is human nature to rank the people in our lives. Nevertheless, when dealing with a church body, it becomes unethical for a leader to favor a member because of how much that member gives, how that member looks, or how influential that member is. We live in a time where there are a lot of people who feel rejected everywhere they go and these people always feel pushed to the back of the line every time someone who's prettier or wealthier than they are shows up. It goes without saying that this leads to church hurt.

(2). Rejecting Members: When a person receives a kidney transplant, that person generally has to stay in the hospital for anywhere between five to ten days. The reason for this is doctors need to make sure that the patient's body does not reject the kidney. Nevertheless, even after the five to ten day window, the body can eventually reject the implanted kidney and when this happens, the immune system will begin to attack that kidney.

This is very similar to how a person feels when they have been or perceive that they have been rejected by their church's leaders. Rejection always hurt, but it can be especially painful when the person who rejects you is a person in authority. This is especially true if the person is someone you look up to. Let's face it: we are flesh-covered creatures; yes, even us leaders. All the same, this does not justify any leader harboring feelings of contempt towards a member that the leader is supposed to be covering. The reality is some people are too immature to be leaders. You can always examine a leader's fruit to determine how mature that leader is, especially when that leader has to lead, communicate, and serve with people he or she simply cannot relate to. Sometimes, we fear what we do not understand and this truth isn't just limited to the congregation. The truth is some leaders simply cannot lead people that they do not understand. This is in no way me trying to excuse their behavior, instead, I'm simply attempting to explain it.

(3). Harboring Unforgiveness: As a child, I hurt myself many times, just like most children.

Everyone with a body has hurt that body at some point in their lives. Most of us have fallen off bicycles, fallen out of trees and gotten into fights with our siblings. We've received many scars in our lives and the same is true for a church body. We hurt one another. But what happens when a leader is hurt or offended by a member and that leader refuses to forgive? The answer is: the leader will repeatedly wound that member.

(4). Subliminal Preaching: Sometimes, an offended and immature leader will use his or her position to publicly and passively rebuke a member of his or her own church. A leader should always respond to ungodly or offensive behavior by directly and privately addressing the offending member. Of course, the leader needs to have another leader with him or her whenever he or she addresses that member. It is always hurtful when a leader grabs the mic and proceeds to intentionally preach sermons designed to hurt or embarrass a co-laborer in the faith, but sadly enough, this does happen.

(5). Public Rebuke: Very much like the previous

pointer, a leader addressing a member publicly can be embarrassing and traumatic for that member. Unlike the previous pointer, when a leader does this, that leader won't try to send subliminal messages from the pulpit. Instead, he or she will publicly address a member or non-member about something he or she did. Of course, there are some cases when a member should be corrected in public or in private, but most corrections should be done outside of the ear-shot of the congregation. A good example is an usher sharply and publicly antagonizing a visitor about something she's wearing. As people grow in the Lord, they'll change from the inside out, but anytime a person is publicly humiliated, that person will likely run away from the church.

(6). Gossip: What you say to your leaders should never be shared with anyone else, but it does happen. Some people have found themselves at the other end of their leaders' gossiping tongues. One of the reasons this is so hurtful is because people often tell their leaders things that they have never told anyone, including their parents, spouses or children. Gossip is always hurtful and any person who's been a victim of gossip, especially gossip from his or her own leader, will suffer with some deep-rooted trust issues.

(7). Slander: Slander normally occurs when a member attempts to leave a church — especially when that member is going to another church where he or she will assume a greater position than he or she did at the previous church. Like gossip, slander can be very traumatizing and damaging to, not only a person's reputation, but it can damage their self-perception, view of authority and ability trust others.

(8). Fraternization: I know that most people don't want to hear this, but leaders should not get too personal with the members. This is one of the most common causes of church hurt. Since the term "fraternization" can be easily misunderstood, I'll say it this way. Leaders should not invite members into their homes or their personal lives, unless, of course, the members are on the leadership team. The more personal a leader is with a member, the less that member will be able to respect or receive from that leader. Additionally, it will be hard for that member to receive correction from the leader in question.

(9). Spiritual Incest: Another cause for a lot of church hurt is when the shepherd gets romantically involved with one of the sheep. This is spiritual incest and it rarely leads to marriage. Instead, it sets the stage for offense and a whole lot of hurt. It even opens the door for lawsuits, sexual harassment claims and a host of other problems.

(10). Abusing Authority: Anytime there is a distribution of power, there is going to be people who abuse that power. The reality is not everyone is mature enough to wear a title or be given any form of authority. Then again, there are some people who can handle small measures of power, but if they are promoted and given a greater level of authority, they will abuse that authority because they are not mature enough to have it. This is why it is important for leaders to pray about people before promoting them.

When the Member is at Fault

Some wounds are real, while others are nothing

short of self-inflicted. It is important to know the nature of your wound so you'll know how to address it. Below are some common mistakes that members and non-members make:

(1). Unmet Expectations: This is the number one reason for church hurt. Unmet expectations can be justified or they can be preposterous. A justified expectation, for example, would be expecting your leader to love, cover and pray for you. An unjustified expectation could be expecting your leader to call you every time you don't show up at church. Leaders have to tend to the flock, plus, manage their own families. It is questionable behavior for a member to miss church and then get angry with the leadership of that church for not reaching out to him or her. Additionally, let's just be honest with ourselves. Some people come to church because they want something from people and not necessarily from God. They want attention, notoriety and someone to listen to their many complaints, and when they realize that the leader is not going to sit and talk with them everyday about their problems, they get upset. The worst part is they are the first people to scream that they've been hurt by the church when, in truth, they want human toilets to relieve themselves on.

(2). Fear or Hatred of Authority: Because of hurt, rejection, abandonment and a host of negative emotions, some people simply fear and/or hate authority. When a believer hates being submitted to an authority figure, that believer will often challenge anyone who holds a position of authority. This is very similar to what takes place in the animal kingdom. Basically, the challenger is demonstrating territorial behaviors in an attempt to assert himself as the alpha male, or if it's a female, she tries to assert herself as the alpha female. People who have these types of strongholds often go into churches attempting to bully the leadership over those churches, but when this does not work, they claim to have been wounded by the church.

(3). Attempting to Usurp Authority: Have you ever had a co-worker who had the same position and title as you, but that co-worker tried to usurp the manager's power? Suddenly, your co-worker was trying to act like your boss. Sadly enough, that same demonic personality tries to make his or her way to church and attempt to pastor or co-pastor whatever church they've entered. Some people are narcissistic, power thirsty souls who go from church to church trying to shove their way to the top. When their antics are exposed and they are rebuked for their ungodly behaviors, they claim to be victims of church hurt.

(4). Sowing Discord: Some people hate authority; some people wrestle with their leaders for power, and then, there are those who simply like to sow discord. These people will ask questions, but not because they want the answer to those questions; they ask them because they want to sow discord. One of the worst members any body can have is a member that does not agree with the head of that body. When, for example, the left leg does not agree with the head of a person, the left leg won't work and the rest of the body will have to carry the weight that the left leg was supposed to carry. The same is true for a church body. Some people develop negative attitudes towards their leaders and when this happens, instead of praying, they will try to get everyone to see the leader the way they see him or her. That's when they'll inundate the leader with questions designed to humiliate, belittle or antagonize that leader. When their antics backfire, they claim to be the victims of church hurt.

(5). Dark Fantasies: We've all heard nightmarish stories about high school kids who've had crushes on their teachers. When their teachers did not reciprocate their affections, many of them falsely accused their teachers of anything from saying something inappropriate to them or making an inappropriate gesture towards them. Of course, there are some pretty bad teachers out there who have tried to take advantage of their students, but then again, there are some students out there who've tried to take advantage of their educators. Somehow, we seem to be remiss of this behavior, thinking that it has not found its way into the church, but it has. Some people have dark fantasies and wrong intentions toward their leaders and when the leader does not reciprocate their affections, it goes without saying that those people will leave that church and falsely accuse their leaders of behaving inappropriately towards them. Consider what happened to Joseph when he was in Potiphar's house.

Genesis 39:7-21 reads: And it came to pass after these things, that his master's wife cast her eyes upon Joseph; and she said, lie with me. But he refused, and said unto his master's wife, "Behold, my master wotteth not what is with me in the house, and he hath committed all that he hath to my hand; there is none greater in this house than I; neither hath he kept back anything from me but thee, because thou art his wife: how then can I do this great wickedness, and sin against God?" And it came to pass, as she spake to Joseph day by day, that he hearkened not unto her, to lie by her, or to be with her. And it came to pass about this time, that Joseph went into the house to do his business; and there was none of the men of the house there within. And she caught him by his garment, saying, "Lie with me," and he left his garment in her hand, and fled, and got him out.

And it came to pass, when she saw that he had left his garment in her hand, and was fled forth, That she called unto the men of her house, and spake unto them, saying, "See, he hath brought in an Hebrew unto us to mock us; he came in unto me to lie with me, and I cried with a loud voice: And it came to pass, when he heard that I lifted up my

voice and cried, that he left his garment with me, and fled, and got him out." And she laid up his garment by her, until his lord came home. And she spake unto him according to these words, saying, the Hebrew servant, which thou hast brought unto us, came in unto me to mock me: And it came to pass, as I lifted up my voice and cried, that he left his garment with me, and fled out.
And it came to pass, when his master heard the words of his wife, which she spake unto him, saying, "After this manner did thy servant to me," that his wrath was kindled. And Joseph's master took him, and put him into the prison, a place where the king's prisoners were bound: and he was there in the prison."
Sure, we'd love to believe that this behavior doesn't take place today, but it does. I'm sure that Potiphar's wife had a whole lot of people who comforted her, but the truth was: she was not the prey; she was the predator.

(6). Jealousy or Competitive Thinking: The bible tells us in Isaiah 14:13-14 that Lucifer said in his heart, "I will ascend into heaven, I will exalt my throne above the stars of God: I will sit also upon the mount of the congregation, in the sides of the north: I will ascend above the heights of the clouds; I will be like the most High." Understand that wherever there is someone in power, there will be someone who covets that power. Consider this story: A twenty-seven year old man is promoted to pastor after his pastor resigns. He's young, energetic and full of the Word of God, but there are other men and women in the congregation who feel entitled to his position. They feel that they are too old and too wise to sit under him, and for this reason, they begin to question and challenge him. Because of jealousy, they begin to compete with the young minister and their goal is to drive him out of the church or get him to resign his position. The sad truth is that this behavior does happen. Just like Lucifer wanted to take God's place, there are people out there who want to take the place of their leaders.

(7). Familiarity: A Syrian named Publius once said, "Familiarity breeds contempt." During my years in ministry, I've seen leaders get too personal and too close with the people they were supposed to be leading and this almost always backfired. Of course, this is more of the leader's fault than it is the member's, but the reality is because of familiarity, many believers have felt rejected, humiliated or disrespected whenever their leaders attempted to correct their behavior. Familiarity takes away a leaders' ability to lead and it opens the door for a myriad of problems. An example of familiarity in the bible occurred between Abram and Lot. Abram was not supposed to take Lot on his journey with him, but he did. As a result, Lot's servants started contending with Abram's servants. Genesis 13:7 reads, "And there was a strife between the herdmen of Abram's cattle and the herdmen of Lot's cattle: and the Canaanite and the Perizzite dwelled then in the land." The reality is that Abram was on assignment and anytime a leader gets too familiar with a member, that member will start to interfere in the leaders' assignment.

(8). Lack of Communication: Your leader cannot read your mind. Most of us know this, but not everyone believes this. The truth is, there are people out there who will come to church, slouch in their seats, ignore everyone around them, pout, and then, get upset with folks for not knowing what was wrong with them. Without warning, they'll leave the church and when questioned about their choice to leave, they will say things like, "I was going through a storm and no one tried to help me." Of course, these individuals will call their frustration "church hurt" and use it to justify leaving the church altogether. Well, here's the issue: no one knew they were going through a storm. You have to communicate with your leaders and if you're not comfortable sharing your personal life details with them, you need to work towards getting comfortable with it. Your pastor cannot read your mind.

(9). Not Knowing How to Leave a Church: Let's face it: some people don't know how to distance themselves from other people without making a dramatic exit. So, for example, a man may decide that he wants to join another church because it's closer to his home, plus, the pastor has promised to give him a position within that church. However, he knows that his leaders or his church depends on him because he has responsibilities within his own church body. He decides within his heart to go ahead and leave his church, but he doesn't know how to approach the leader or resign peacefully. Every relationship he's ever been in ended dramatically and for this reason, he thinks he needs to make a dramatic exit. So, he looks for something to accuse the leaders or the members about so that he can justify his exit. Believe it or not, this happens more often than most people are aware of. Some people are afraid of being questioned or seeing the disappointed look in their leaders' face, so they opt for a more dramatic exit than a simple resignation letter. Of course, these people will claim to have been hurt by their former churches.

(10). Refusing to Accept Correction: One of the hardest things for a leader to do is correct one of his or her members. However, correction is necessary for growth. The bible details many men of God who were rebuked and those men included: David (after he'd had Uriah killed to be with Bathsheba) and Peter (after he cut off the ear of the high priest's servant, plus, Peter was rebuked by Paul because he would eat with the Gentiles, but whenever he saw circumcised men (Jews), he would separate himself from the Gentiles). When you are a member of a body, you should expect to be corrected whenever necessary. Howbeit, a lot of today's believers hate correction and will publicly ridicule any leader who's tried to privately rebuke them. Remember what the Word says about hating correction. Proverbs 15:32 reads, "He that refuseth instruction despiseth his own soul: but he that heareth reproof getteth understanding."

Of course, there are many unlisted reasons for church hurt, but the root of them all is flesh that has not been submitted to God. Whether the leader is at fault or one of the members is at fault, it is important that we learn to respect one another, follow protocol and lean to the Word of God to see how to handle any issues that arise within the body of Christ. Matthew 21:26 (NIV) instructs us this way: "'You have heard that it was said to the people long ago, 'You shall not murder, and anyone who murders will be subject to judgment.' But I tell you that anyone who is angry with a brother or sister will be subject to judgment. Again, anyone who says to a brother or sister, 'Raca,' is answerable to the court. And anyone who says, 'You fool!' will be in danger of the fire of hell. Therefore, if you are offering your gift at the altar and there remember that your brother or sister has something against you, leave your gift there in front of the altar. First go and be reconciled to them; then come and offer your gift. Settle matters quickly with your adversary who is taking you to court. Do it while you are still together on the way, or your adversary may hand you over to the judge, and the judge may hand you over to the officer, and you may be thrown into prison. Truly I tell you, you will not get out until you have paid the last penny.'"

Unrealistic Expectations

As mentioned in the previous chapter, one of the most common reasons for church hurt is unmet expectations, otherwise known as unrealistic expectations. Now, this isn't to say that all expectations are bad, but it is to say that many people come to church expecting time and resources that the church, quite frankly, simply does not have to give. The same is true for leadership, of course. Many leaders expect far too much from the people who are serving under them. When unrealistic expectations are in the midst of any relationship, that relationship becomes an expensive burden.

Pastor John had just met the newest member of the church he was pastoring. Her name was Vicky and she was a single mother of two adult children. Vicky's youngest son had just left home to go to college, so she was rather lonely.

From the beginning, Pastor John and his wife, Jane,

knew that Vicky was going to be somewhat of a burden. Nevertheless, they reasoned within themselves that this (carrying the burden of others) was what the church was for. However, after a few months, the husband and wife team were now reconsidering their positions.

Before attending Pastor John's church, Vicky had attended three churches in the span of a year and she'd been kicked out of them all. At first, the Smith's reasoned within themselves that each church had been cruel and ill-equipped to deal with a person like Vicky, after all, she was pushy, domineering, opinionated and very emotional. This was the evidence that Vicky was a wounded soul and the Smiths were determined to help her heal. Time would tell, however, that Vicky wasn't interested in healing; she simply wanted attention.

Vicky would show up to every bible study class and disrupt the class by constantly raising her hand and asking questions. The problem wasn't in her asking questions; the problem was that Vicky didn't really want the answer to the questions she asked. She simply wanted to voice her opinion. Vicky's

Unrealistic Expectations

disruptions were so bad that the young woman (Barbara) who'd initially taught bible study classes resigned. Of course, Vicky tried to volunteer to teach the class, but Pastor John told her that she wasn't ready yet and this was true. With no one left to teach the class, co-Pastor Jane decided to take over temporarily. It was during her first class that she saw the extent of Vicky's venom.

It was a Tuesday evening and class was scheduled to start in less than fifteen minutes. Pastor Jane was coming out of her office when she came face to face with Vicky. "Pastor, I need to talk with you and it can't wait," said Vicky. The good pastor looked at her watch. "Class starts in 12 minutes," she said to Vicky. "I know," replied Vicky. "This won't take long." From there, Vicky started complaining about another church member. Her complaint was that Betty, the church's secretary, had not passed her call through to Pastor Jane's office when she'd called. After Pastor Jane explained that Betty was just doing her job, Vicky went on to complain about Betty's attitude towards her. "I saw her in the foyer the other day and she did not speak at all," complained Vicky. "I don't know if she has a

147

Unrealistic Expectations

problem with me or not, but I don't like feeling like I'm being picked on." Pastor Jane looked at her watch. There were three minutes left until class. "I don't think she's picking, Vicky. She may have been in deep thought. Betty is a real nice person if you get to know her." Vicky was unrelenting. "I understand," she said. "I'll give her the benefit of the doubt this time, but I do expect her to come out of her deep thought to at least speak. After all, this is supposed to be God's house." Pastor Jane could feel herself getting anxious. "Vicky, this isn't a big deal; class is about to start. I gotta go." Vicky touched Jane's arm. "I understand. The problem could be me. I've been dealing with a lot of severe depression and my doctor says that I need to take it easy, but it's hard to do so. My own children don't call me too much; my daughters have absolutely nothing to do with me. And did I tell you that my dad, God rest his soul, used to beat me till I was black and blue? I have so much on my plate and it's overwhelming..." Pastor Jane had to cut Vicky off. "Class is starting now, Vicky. Maybe you can arrange a counseling session soon — if that's what you need." With that, Pastor Jane walked away, even though Vicky continued to talk.

Unrealistic Expectations

In class, Vicky seemed withdrawn at first. It was clear to Pastor Jane that Vicky had taken offense with the fact that she'd walked off. Nevertheless, Vicky knew that classes were about to start and she didn't care. Howbeit, thirty minutes into class and Vicky was back to being her intrusive self. She kept raising her hand and instead of asking simple questions, she'd ask a question and then, proceed to give her opinion. Vicky would talk non-stop until Pastor Jane cut her off. This happened four times until Pastor Jane had had enough. "Vicky," said Pastor Jane. "If you have a question; ask it. Don't give us your take on it. This class only lasts an hour and there are other people here who have questions." Unmoved by Pastor Jane's rebuke, Vicky cut in. "I thought that's what bible study was for; I thought it was for questions. I'm sorry if I'm disruptive to your little class, but if I have a question, I'm gonna ask it." Pastor Jane closed her bible and turned her body towards Vicky. "No, you will not. You will ask a single question and that's it. If you have an opinion, post it on your Facebook page. You're not the teacher here; you have to remember that." Vicky was argumentative. She boasted about teaching Sunday school at her last

149

Unrealistic Expectations

church and regardless of what Pastor Jane said to her, she would not stop talking. In that moment, it became very clear why Vicky had been kicked out of three churches. She didn't come to church to learn; she came to dominate, and when she did not get her way, she became argumentative and confrontational. "The First Amendment gives me the freedom of speech and I'm going to use it! If you try to stop me, I'll sue you and this church!" shouted Vicky. Pastor Jane lowered her head. "Leave," she said to Vicky. "What?" Vicky sat down in her chair. "What did you say to me?" Pastor Jane lifted her head and looked Vicky directly in her eyes. "Vicky, please leave this building and do not come back." Pastor Jane pointed to the door, but Vicky refused to move. Instead, she began to manifest her wicked heart all the more. Vicky laughed, mocked the pastor and even kept addressing the shocked members every time Pastor Jane told her to leave. Another member stood to his feet. "Pastor Jane? Do you want me to put her out?" asked Deacon Mark. Pastor Jane knew this wasn't a good idea; Vicky would only assault Deacon Mark and then claim she'd been assaulted. "No, said Pastor Jane. "Call the police." When Deacon Mark started grabbing for his

150

Unrealistic Expectations

cell phone, Vicky suddenly stood to her feet. "I'll leave on my own! You guys don't know what you're talking about, anyhow! I see why this church is so small; no one wants to come here! Stupid!" Vicky made her way out of the church, screaming and swearing as she went.

Vicky went on to post negative reviews about Pastor John's church online and she would always cast herself as a victim of church hurt to anyone who was willing to listen to her. By the close of that year, Vicky had been kicked out of two more churches and she'd even been arrested for assaulting one of the leaders at another church.

Now, some people would say that it was wrong for Pastor Jane to make Vicky leave, but what was she to do? The truth is — Vicky didn't come to church to learn; she came to take over. This is a great example of unrealistic expectations. Vicky wanted the church to heal her, pity her and give her the mic. She didn't care about her fellow church members; she cared only about herself. People like Vicky will talk non-stop about their problems — problems that they don't really want help with. They talk just to hear

151

themselves talk and to figure out what they want to do. They will rarely, if ever, accept and apply the advice that their leaders give them. Honestly, it would be a blessing if the leader can get a word in. The point is — some people hurt the church; they aren't necessarily hurt by it.

Pastor John and his wife, Jane, were the victims here. They endured Vicky's intrusive, disrespectful ways and they endured the lies she'd told about them after she was asked to leave their church. Gentle souls themselves, the couple felt disappointed that they'd come across a person they felt they could not help.

Imagine if someone told Vicky they were writing a book about church hurt and were collecting testimonies. Could you imagine the salacious tale she'd weave about Pastor John, his wife, and the other churches she'd been kicked out of? Regarding Pastors John and Jane, she would likely say that Pastor John was flirtatious and because of this, Pastor Jane was jealous of her. She'd cast herself as an innocent member who was simply looking for a church to call home, but anyone who got to know

Unrealistic Expectations

her would come to see her, not for who she really is, but for the evil that's lurking within her. The point here is that church hurt affects leaders too, especially when people come into the church with unrealistic expectations.

One of the problems with unrealistic expectations is that people who have them generally have a sold-out, tunnel-eyed view of the church. They believe that the church has a certain responsibility to them and others, and when this responsibility is not met, they become angry — sometimes, even vengeful. This isn't because the church did not fulfill its obligations. The problem is the individual had unrealistic expectations in regards to the church. For example, Vicky wanted to be heard; she wanted her church's undivided attention. She wanted to control the church by controlling the pastors. She wanted to be feared and esteemed. Her attitude was nothing short of demonic. However, leaders can have unrealistic expectations too and this happens more often than we care to talk about.

Diablo had been the pastor at his church for more than four years. One of the youngest members in his

Unrealistic Expectations

fellowship, Diablo put a lot of pressure on himself to keep up with his fellow pastors. For this reason, Diablo was very hard on his ministry team — so much so that more than twenty people had resigned from the church he pastored in less than two years. He was known for his unprofessional outbursts and emotional tantrums.

One of the leaders in Diablo's church was named Mr. Frank. Mr. Frank was an elderly man who'd pastored a church for more than thirty years, but after having endured a series of health challenges, Mr. Frank retired from preaching. Years later, the church he'd once pastored closed its doors for good and Mr. Frank found himself in need of a good church home. After watching a television commercial that Diablo had done promoting the church, Mr. Frank was sure he'd found the place he was meant to worship at.

Mr. Frank joined the ministry team because he wanted to help out around the church. He was used to being active in ministry and he wanted to remain active. For this reason, he signed up for the ministry team at Diablo's church and he was soon promoted as a deacon. However, two other ministers in training quit and left the church altogether because of Diablo's quick temper and unreasonable demands. This left Mr. Frank as the remaining deacon, but he didn't mind at all. He was used to hard work. However, many people in the church noticed how hard Diablo seemed to be with Mr. Frank; he was merciless and didn't take Mr. Frank's age or health into consideration.

During one Sunday service, Diablo's frustration was on full display for the entire congregation to see. He complained about not having sufficient help with his ministry and he talked about Pastor Donnie, a leader in the fellowship he was a part of, having a brand new state of the art website. "No one here has ever volunteered to help the church with a website," complained Diablo. "I guess y'all think that I'm supposed to preach and pay for everything. Well, if that's what you're thinking, you're wrong! As long as we've been active, we should have a logo, a website, brochures — you name it!" After his rant, Pastor Diablo concluded his sermon and said the normal benediction. No one came to the front to get saved, rededicate their life to Christ or join Diablo's church. Instead, there was a noticeable silence in the place, and if Diablo's pulpit rant hadn't been enough, members were horrified when they noticed that he had Mr. Frank carrying a heavy tote bag that belonged to him. The worst part was Mr. Frank was noticeably struggling with Diablo's bag, nevertheless, he was determined to carry it to its destination.

One of the male congregants (Jason) stopped Diablo and offered to design the church's website, but when Diablo sent him the outline for the site he wanted, Jason soon realized that Diablo wanted something that was far outside of his expertise. He wanted a top notch, hard-to-design website for free. He wanted the site to be far better than Pastor Donnie's site. Jason sent the details to other web designers and developers to see how much they'd charge to design the site, but no one was willing to design it for less than $25,000. Again, the amount of work that Diablo wanted was astronomical. After a few days of trying to design the site, Jason realized that he'd bitten off more than he could chew. He decided to contact Pastor Diablo and let him know that he could not design such an extravagant site.

Unrealistic Expectations

The phone rang and Jason could feel his hands trembling. How would Pastor Diablo respond? Jason regretted volunteering without hearing the full details. "Hello, Pastor. This is Jason. Anyhow, after reviewing the details of what you want, I've come to realize that this project is too complex for me. I've contacted other designers to get pricing, but most people want six figures to design the site. The cheapest designer I came across wanted twenty-five grand. Call me back when you can." Jason was relieved that he'd gotten the pastor's voicemail, but before he could celebrate, his phone chimed, letting him know that he had a new text message. It was from Pastor Diablo. "I don't care what it costs! Get it done!" Jason was confused. He didn't have that kind of money. What did Pastor Diablo mean? Was he willing to pay that kind of money? Jason called the pastor's phone again, but still, there was no answer. After that, he decided to text him. "What do you mean? I don't have that kind of money. I'm just a student." Jason waited for fifteen minutes to receive a response and when it came in, it was even more confusing than the first one. "No, I'm not paying for anything! You said you could do it so get it done! I'm in a meeting. Figure it out and get it done. That's all I can tell you."

Three weeks went by and Jason was still working on the front page of the site because Pastor Diablo kept rejecting every new design he presented. On top of that, Mr. Frank's health seemed to be deteriorating, but Pastor Diablo would not let up off him. Eventually, Mr. Frank had to be bedridden and to his surprise, he didn't get so much as a call or a text message from Pastor Diablo.

Pastor Diablo never got the site he wanted. He kept ridiculing and harassing Jason until he changed his number and stopped attending Pastor Diablo's church altogether. Mr. Frank recovered from his illness, but also decided to find another church home. Pastor Diablo was eventually demoted by his overseer because his wife had a miscarriage and was hospitalized after the pastor had allegedly attacked her. During counseling through his church, Pastor Diablo's overseer was able to determine that he was obviously not graced for the position he had. He dreamed of having a mega church and an entourage of followers who hung on to his every word, and for this reason, he placed unrealistic expectations on his congregation and ministry team.

Unrealistic expectations are one of the main culprits behind church hurt because we, as humans, tend to measure the loyalty of others by our own convictions and strengths. For example, let's say that Mr. Frank found himself a new church home that's being pastored by a man named Bishop Doe. Bishop Doe has had quite a few ministers to leave his church and he's not completely over it yet. Mr. Frank comes in and tells his story regarding how Pastor Diablo treated him. Immediately, Bishop Doe's beliefs take over and he begins to berate Mr. Frank for leaving. "That's what's wrong with half of these churches today," he says. "No loyalty left. Folks get offended and quit on you the minute you try to correct them. When I was under my former Bishop, he offended me many times, but I didn't leave." The bishop is judging Mr. Frank unfairly. The rule he's using to measure the man of God is his own hurt, experience and convictions. When we do this to others, we completely disregard their experiences and convictions and we replace them with our own. This only causes us to hurt others and eventually, our churches become ghost towns.

Another example of unrealistic expectations, although subtle, took place in the life of a young, Catholic man. Joshua had been brought up Catholic and, of course, since that was his family's background, that was the path he'd decided to choose for himself. Nevertheless, he was open to visiting and worshiping with other denominations.

According to Joshua, he'd visited two churches outside his denomination, with one of them being a trinitarian church and the other being a non-denominational church. In both churches, according to Joshua, he'd been offended. Now, the offense was not with the denominations because the denominations as a whole had nothing to do with the behaviors of the leaders who'd offended Joshua. The offense had everything to do with the leaders' publicly pressuring him during Sunday service to join their churches. Joshua said that one of them had even spoken about the possibility of him going to hell. Of course, this pressure and the pastor's cruel words did not scare Joshua into joining their churches. Instead, it justified his belief that Catholicism was the safest label for him to wear. Now, I'm not sure how many times Joshua had attended both churches before he'd been offended, but what I do know is this is the wrong approach to winning souls for Christ.

Some leaders are so hard-pressed to get new members that they pressure their visitors with scare tactics and cunning words, and this is ungodly. The leaders should have kept teaching and preaching in love, and when Joshua felt led by God to join the church, he would have gotten up on his own. Now, for many of you, this may not sound like church hurt, but it is. These events were so traumatic to the young man that he stopped visiting churches outside his denomination, fearing that he'd be humiliated yet again by some overly anxious pastor. The point is that unrealistic expectations ruin ministries.

The Concept of Marriage

Ephesians 5:25-30 reads, "Husbands, love your wives, as Christ loved the church and gave himself up for her, that he might sanctify her, having cleansed her by the washing of water with the word, so that he might present the church to himself in splendor, without spot or wrinkle or any such thing, that she might be holy and without blemish. In the same way husbands should love their wives as their own bodies. He who loves his wife loves himself. For no one ever hated his own flesh, but nourishes and cherishes it, just as Christ does the church, because we are members of his body."

Divorce can be painfully traumatic because of the level of investment (both emotional and financial) that most people put into their marriages. People tend to choose their spouses based on their own personal needs, meaning, they believe that the institution of marriage or the individuals that they intend to marry has something to add to their lives.

Normal people don't get married thinking they'll end up divorced. Most people get married with the intent to stay married. However, trials come, disagreements rise up and hurtful words are released. Suddenly, one or both parties involved no longer feels that the person they are married to is adding to them; instead, both parties start believing that their spouses are taking from them. This happens until they finally start feeling emotionally depleted and defeated. It is when a person feels that he or she has nothing left to give that the topic of divorce is suddenly brought up. This is very similar to church hurt.

Most people who've been hurt by their church, especially by the people they entrusted to lead and cover them, say that leaving their churches felt like a bad divorce. And this isn't surprising, considering the level of emotional and financial investments that most people give to their churches. Just like most people don't marry with the intent to divorce, the average person doesn't join a church with the intent to resign. Most people join churches because they believe that the institution they've chosen has something that they need. In other words, people choose church homes that they believe can and will add to them, but people leave their church homes when they feel that the church is bankrupting them.

All non-romantic relationships can be compared to marriages. For example, in a friendship, each party has certain obligations to fulfill. Both parties are expected to be nice, patient, loving, understanding and non-judgmental. Additionally, both parties expect one another to make a few sacrifices for the friendship — sacrifices like answering the phone in times of trouble or helping one another out when possible. When one or both parties do not comply with the "friendship code" that's been assumed, offense comes in and the friendship takes a hit. This won't end the friendship in most cases, but it will damage it. The same is true for our relationships on the church-front.

I have been married for over thirty years, so it goes without saying, that my wife and I have offended one another a lot over the course of our lives. There was a time when we'd both even considered divorcing each other, but only because we placed greater value on what we wanted from the marriage than we did for the marriage itself. This means that we were prideful, stubborn and unwilling to compromise, but glory be to God, we had wise counsel to help us get past the mindsets that were sabotaging our marriage. Nevertheless, we have still continued to offend one another from time to time, and that's just a part of being the imperfect creatures that we are. Our flaws keep us humble and remind us that we need Jesus, regardless of our titles and honors.

To maintain our marriage, we had to come to understand order, plus, we had to come to the understanding that neither of us are perfect. I had to learn to respect her opinion and she had to do the same for me, but more importantly, we both had to learn to apply the Word of God to our marriage. After we learned the value of order, respect and honor, we were then qualified to be leaders in the Lord's church. The reason is — we had to apply that same principle to our ministerial assignment, meaning, we both had to understand that we were going to come in contact with people from all walks of life. This means that we first had to learn to be bilingual in regards to our love language towards one another before we could become multilingual in regards to our love for others. It sounds easy enough, but it isn't because we had to constantly learn to put away ourselves so that the churches we led would operate in unity.

The concept of marriage is that everyone who gets married will become one flesh with the person they marry. However, marriage is not stable until the couple becomes one mind with one another. This doesn't mean that they agree on all things; it means that each marital unit must be in agreement in regards to the overall goal of their marriage. That goal must be more important than the pettiness that arises in marriages. Think of it this way. You're at a car dealership looking at a few cars and you come in contact with another potential buyer who is obnoxious and unpleasant to be around. Mark is pompous, narcissistic and just plain rude. He lacks tact and he keeps saying some of the most obnoxious things to the women who pass him by. Suddenly, a salesman's voice comes on the intercom and he announces that the contest is about to begin and that every person interested in participating is to rush to the front desk and sign up within the next

The Concept of Marriage

five minutes. Curious, you ask Mark what the contest is about and he tells you. "They are gonna give away two brand new cars. To win one of the cars, each person will be paired up with a random stranger and they must both place their hands on whichever car the dealer tells them to place their hands on. The pair who doesn't move their hands from the car will win a car each." Excited, you rush to the desk to sign up, and a few minutes later, a woman emerges from the back room and stands in front of the growing crowd. She announces the contestants and who they'll be paired with. To your surprise, your name is announced, but to your disgust, you're being paired with Mark. You desperately need that car, but the idea of standing a few feet away from Mark for hours, or possibly days at a time, sounds unreasonable to you. Nevertheless, you decide to accept the challenge because again, you desperately need a car and you can't afford one.

The contest begins and Mark starts being his obnoxious self almost immediately. He swears a lot and he won't stop talking about himself. In the first few hours, you find yourself wanting to remove

The Concept of Marriage

your hand from the car so you can knock Mark off his feet, but the overall goal of winning the car is far bigger to you than your desire to silence Mark. "Be quiet, please," you say to Mark. "I need peace at this moment." Mark is offended. With his right hand still firmly placed on the car, he moves closer to you and begins to swear at you. You turn your head, hoping that he'll leave you alone, but this only seems to further enrage him. To make matters worse, Mark has one of the worst cases of halitosis that you've ever encountered. Why oh why did the dealer pair him with you? For a brief moment, you consider head-butting Mark, but every time you look at the car, you are reminded why you are doing what you are doing. So, you choose to ignore Mark and move away from him, hoping that he'll finish his angry rant and find something else to talk about. After all, it's become painfully obvious to you that regardless of how long this contest lasts, Mark is not going to stop talking. What are you going to do to stay in it? A wise man or woman would simply use the overall goal of winning the car as their focal point. Mark would just be a bump in the road. You see, your goal isn't just to keep your hands on the car, but it is to encourage Mark to keep his hands on the car as well. Offending him will only serve to work against the both of you, but encouraging him will help you to meet your overall goal. The same is true for the marriage unit. You won't always like your spouse, but if you place your eyes on the overall goal (to please God), you'll learn to crucify your flesh. We must also apply this concept to the church unit.

You are married to your church family. To be married means to be united or paired up. What if God told you that the uncomfortable church that you once went to was actually the garden He chose to grow you in, despite the church hurt, the obnoxious members and the easily offended pastor? Now, make no mistake about what I'm saying — I'm in no way implying that you should return to a church that you've left, but what I am saying is that sometimes, we have to take into consideration that God intentionally places us in uncomfortable situations so that we can learn to focus on His overall agenda. What is His agenda? It's simple: to win souls for the kingdom of God. This means that some of what we call church hurt is nothing but God stretching us; He's teaching us to get over ourselves so that we can see the bigger picture.

Of course, just like natural marriages, there are some religious relationships that were not put together by God. They are the products of voids, lack of understanding and convenience. However, when a body of believers try to come together outside of God's will, that body's function will be irregular. There will be too many people trying to operate as the head and too many people trying to function in roles that God did not grace them to perform. This leads to frustration and a whole lot of church hurt. However, just like marriages that were not put together by God, religious relationships that were not put together by God must pass God's tests. The people who've come together must humble themselves, love each other, forgive one another and learn to work together. Once that family unit learns the power of love and how to apply it, God will begin to start to use them where they are or place them in the church units that He wants them to function in. Understand this: your church needs your function, just like a husband needs his wife and vice versa.

A pride-filled husband can easily say that because he pays all the bills at his home that he does not need his wife. If he were to lose her, however, he would slowly come to realize how valuable she is to him and how vital she is to his survival. He may not realize it, but she may be the very reason he's excited to get up and go to work each day. She may be the very reason that he tolerates the job he has. She may be the very reason he showers everyday and she may be the pillar behind his healthy lifestyle. Without her, he may find himself an unkempt, overweight man who hates his job and is buried in bills. The point is — despite what he believes, every husband needs his wife! The same is true for the body of believers that God wants you to be a part of. They need you and you need them. Without them, you may find yourself entertaining a lot of fruitless friendships and relationships with people who want to take from you, but are not willing to give. Every relationship is a give and take. When we're in the right relationships, the give and the take are balanced, but when we're in the wrong relationships, we'll find ourselves giving more than we're receiving. This imbalance is the evidence that we are not connected to the right body of believers.

The Taste Test

Have you ever mistaken an orange for an apple or a peach for a banana? Chances are, you haven't and the most obvious reason is: you know the differences between each fruit visually. Howbeit, if you were to do a taste test blindfolded, you'd still be able to determine which fruit you were eating. This is because every fruit has its own unique taste and texture.

Ironically enough, there are some fruits that look alike and some even taste similar. For example, oranges and tangerines look almost the same. Their tastes are even similar, but there are some noticeable differences between the two. Tangerines tend to be smaller, sweeter and have a somewhat flatter taste than oranges. Obviously, oranges are more acidic, tart and slightly bigger than mandarins. Then again, grapefruits look similar to oranges, but are noticeably larger and tarter than oranges. The interior of grapefruits are different as well; they tend to have a redder appearance than oranges. So, even though fruits can be different, there are some that look the same and even taste similar, but if you've experienced them all, you will be able to tell the differences either by looking at them or experiencing them. The same is true when dealing with false prophets.

Matthew 7:15-20 reads, "Beware of false prophets, who come to you in sheep's clothing but inwardly are ravenous wolves. You will recognize them by their fruits. Are grapes gathered from thornbushes, or figs from thistles? So, every healthy tree bears good fruit, but the diseased tree bears bad fruit. A healthy tree cannot bear bad fruit, nor can a diseased tree bear good fruit. Every tree that does not bear good fruit is cut down and thrown into the fire. Thus you will recognize them by their fruits" (ESV). One of the issues we see arising in today's church is a lot of people claim to be prophets of God. And let's be real with ourselves — not everyone who says they are prophets are actually prophets. Nevertheless, people are proclaiming their own names, titles and righteousness, and from there, they are proceeding to launch ministries. These people have no overseer, meaning, they have no oversight and no one to correct them. It goes without saying that such individuals have done a great deal of injustice to the body of Christ.

One of the reasons we all need someone to correct us is — it is only natural for us, as humans, to think we're right all the time when, in truth, we are all flawed creatures. Having someone to examine us helps us to stay humble and it encourages us to examine ourselves. For example, leaders who have no overseer are less likely to consider whether what they say may be offensive to others. For this reason, it's easy for pride to set in and cause them to believe that their lack of tact is actually holy boldness when, in truth, it's nothing but a boisterous display of human emotions. Without a doubt, leaders like this are known to hurt their followers repeatedly and this is why some churches will go from having one hundred members to having a mere ten members. The problem, in this case, isn't the sheep; it's the shepherd. Now, this does not mean that every prophet who doesn't have a leader is a false prophet, but what it does mean is that leaders who have no overseers tend to behave like false prophets.

Let's reexamine Matthew 7:15-20, which tells us to beware of false prophets. Google defines the word "beware" this way: be cautious and alert to the dangers of. Another word for "beware" is "be aware," which means to be knowledgeable of. So, another way to translate the scripture would be, "Be cautiously knowledgeable of false prophets" or "Do not be ignorant regarding the deeds and ways of false prophets."

Another thing that Matthew 7 tells us is that false prophets are like ravenous wolves wearing sheep's clothing. The word "ravenous" means extremely hungry, therefore, a false prophet is like an extremely hungry wolf disguised as a sheep. This helps to explain 1 Peter 5:8, which reads, "Be sober-minded; be watchful. Your adversary the devil prowls around like a roaring lion, seeking someone to devour" (ESV). In Matthew 7, we read about ravenous wolves and in 1 Peter 5, we hear that the enemy is looking for someone to devour. Interestingly enough, the Lord is using what we do understand to explain the ways of the enemy. Satan is desperate to consume us, however, the bible tells us that we will know Satan's children (false prophets) by their fruit, meaning, we too have to experience them.

1 Peter 5 says that Satan is looking for someone to devour, meaning, he cannot devour everyone. He has to find someone who is edible or, in other words, not submitted to God. He deplores false prophets to come among believers, pretending to be believers themselves. When false prophets rise to leadership, they begin to devour God's people one church hurt, one misquoted scripture and one false prophecy at a time. This is why church hurt has risen to become the epidemic it is today. It's not because of godly leaders who were chosen by God to teach His Word; it's because of ungodly, self-appointed leaders who have ordained themselves or been ordained by other ungodly or non-sober leaders — who've been led astray by selfish ambition.

The Taste Test

One of the most common questions (obviously) is: how do I tell the difference between a true prophet of God versus a false prophet? The answer is simple: conduct the taste test. False prophets are led by their flesh and of course, they are led by the enemy; whereas, true prophets are led by the Spirit of God. What you have to examine is each prophet's fruit or, a better way of saying it is — you have to examine and acknowledge what each prophet is producing. Galatians 5:19-24 gives us the recipe for false prophets, and it reads, "Now the works of the flesh are evident: sexual immorality, impurity, sensuality, idolatry, sorcery, enmity, strife, jealousy, fits of anger, rivalries, dissensions, divisions, envy, drunkenness, orgies, and things like these. I warn you, as I warned you before, that those who do such things will not inherit the kingdom of God" (ESV).

Sexual immorality: We've all read about the scandals happening in many churches where the leaders have been sleeping with the members or they've left their wives to be with other women. How can a prophet hear from God regarding you, but be completely deaf to the voice of God regarding himself or herself? Anyone who has not mastered their own flesh should not be on the pulpit. Matthew 4:3 (NLT) says it this way, "And why worry about a speck in your friend's eye when you have a log in your own?"

Impurity: Obviously, the root word of "impurity" is "purity," which means to be undefiled or free of contamination. To be impure means to be contaminated by the cares of this world. Mark 4:13-20 warns us this way, "And he said unto them, 'Know ye not this parable? And how then will ye know all parables? The sower soweth the word. And these are they by the way side, where the word is sown; but when they have heard, Satan cometh immediately, and taketh away the word that was sown in their hearts. And these are they likewise which are sown on stony ground; who, when they have heard the word, immediately receive it with gladness; and have no root in themselves, and so endure but for a time: afterward, when affliction or persecution ariseth for the word's sake, immediately they are offended. And these are they which are sown among thorns; such as hear the word, and the cares of this world, and the deceitfulness of riches, and the lusts of other things entering in, choke the word, and it becometh unfruitful. And these are they which are sown on good ground; such as hear the word, and receive it, and bring forth fruit, some thirtyfold, some sixty, and some an hundred." What these scriptures are telling us is that people who were once pure become contaminated when they have stony hearts, are easily offended and they are led astray by riches or the cares of this world. Understand this: they still have the Word in them, but there is some ungodliness in them that causes them to become impure.

Sensuality: Merriam-Webster defines the word "sensual" this way: "relating to or consisting in the gratification of the senses or the indulgence of appetite." Of course, we know that the fives senses are: smell, taste, sight, touch and hearing. In other words, sensuality means to be led (astray) by the flesh. A false prophet is led by his or her flesh. False prophets cannot endure the tests of a storm because they have no faith to sustain them. Instead, they believe what they hear, see, feel, smell and taste. Sure, some false prophets can display signs and wonders, but this is not done by faith in God; it's a display of witchcraft. Consider the slave girl who followed Paul and Silas. Acts 16:16-18 tells the story this way: "As we were going to the place of prayer, we were met by a slave girl who had a spirit of divination and brought her owners much gain by fortune-telling. She followed Paul and us, crying out,

'These men are servants of the Most High God, who proclaim to you the way of salvation.' And this she kept doing for many days. Paul, having become greatly annoyed, turned and said to the spirit, 'I command you in the name of Jesus Christ to come out of her.' And it came out that very hour" (ESV). Now, if Paul didn't have any discernment, he could have easily labeled the woman a prophetess and asked her to walk with them and people would have believed that she was a woman of God. She would have, instead, been a false prophet.

Idolatry: Idolatry is the worship of other gods; it means to have an idol or, better yet, a false god. The Greek word, according to Strong's Concordance, for "idolatry" is "eidólolatria" and it is translated to mean: worship or service of an image (definition taken from Strong's Concordance). A false prophet does not worship Jehovah; instead, false prophets often worship themselves, money, fame, power and anything this world has to offer.

Sorcery: Merriam-Webster defines "sorcery" this way: "The use of power gained from the assistance or control of evil spirits especially for divining." In other words, the spirit or spirits behind false prophets are evil spirits; we know them as demons.

False prophets use evil spirits to acquire the knowledge and false prophecies they use to lead others astray. This is why God told us to test the spirits. 1 John 4:1 reads, "Beloved, do not believe every spirit, but test the spirits to see whether they are from God, for many false prophets have gone out into the world."

Enmity: Enmity is strife. Google defines "enmity" this way: "The state or feeling of being actively opposed or hostile to someone or something." A great example of enmity is racism. If your leader is a racist, your leader is a false prophet because hatred and love cannot coexist. 1 John 4:20 (ESV) reads, "If anyone says, "I love God," and hates his brother, he is a liar; for he who does not love his brother whom he has seen cannot love God whom he has not seen." We are to hate what God hates and love what God loves, but false prophets often take up causes that do not edify the body of Christ, and by doing so, they sow strife and discord.

Strife: Strife means conflict. Patheos.org says this about "strife": "Vigorous or bitter conflict, discord, or antagonism toward someone else or others. Strife could include being in a quarrel, struggle, or clash with others or another person and might even include an armed conflict, but is not limited to being in competition or rivalry with someone else or with others. Strife sometimes includes a bitter and even violent disagreement even with those who are in authority." Strife can best be described as the lack of love and a demonstration of that lack of love. It is centered around selfish ambition, pride and jealousy.

Jealousy: Jealousy is covetous; it means to covet what someone else has. It means to resent someone inwardly or obviously because of what that person has, will have, or your perception of that person. Because false prophets are led astray by the cares of this world, they are, by default, jealous creatures and this leads them to be cruel. Song of Solomon 8:6 says, "Set me as a seal upon your heart, as a seal upon your arm, for love is strong as death, jealousy is fierce as the grave. Its flashes are flashes of fire, the very flame of the LORD" (ESV). Jealous people are merciless, slanderous and oftentimes murderous.

Fits of Anger: Fits of anger can best be described as temper tantrums. It can best be described as compulsive behavior brought on by rage; for example, let's say that a man named Howard was having a bad day. He got a traffic citation on his way to work, his daughter got suspended from school and his wife won't stop complaining about the unpaid bills. Howard arrives home after getting the citation and immediately, his wife asks him if he stopped to pay the energy bill. "No," he says. "I got a ticket, so I came straight home." His wife lets out a loud sigh and then starts to scream at him. Howard bites his lip and starts to clinch his fit. Without warning, he suddenly leaps to his feet and begins to beat his wife. For an entire minute and a half, Howard swings mercilessly at his wife, pulling her hair and dragging her as he strikes her. After the beating, he runs throughout the house, pulling pictures off the wall and breaking anything that looks breakable. This is an example of a fit of rage. False prophets tend to exhibit this behavior whenever they are overwhelmed.

Rivalries: Google defines "rivalry" this way: "Competition for the same objective or for superiority in the same field." What would a false prophet compete for? It's obvious: attention, power, platforms and money. As believers, we are all playing for the same team, which means that no competition should be found among us. However, false prophets compete with true prophets because they covet their platforms.

Dissensions: A dissension is a disagreement that leads to quarreling, discord and contention. Matthew 5:25 tells us how to handle disagreements, and it reads, "Agree with thine adversary quickly, whiles thou art in the way with him; lest at any time the adversary deliver thee to the judge, and the judge deliver thee to the officer, and thou be cast into prison." Now, this doesn't mean that if someone is trying to get you to lie that you should lie or if someone is trying to get you to sin that you should sin. Instead, it simply means that for the sake of peace, just go ahead and agree with your enemy. For example, if your cousin borrowed money from you and because he doesn't want to repay you, he starts to speak harshly to you, the best thing for you to do is forgive him the debt. Call him over the phone and tell him not to worry about the debt he owes you. This is how forgiveness works. God will see to it that you receive every penny back that was taken from you, if you cast that burden upon Him. If you don't forgive your cousin, quarreling will ensue and you will never see the money.

Divisions: Divisions are cliquish behaviors. It

simply means to be at odds with other believers, whether they be a part of the church body that you are a part of or they be a part of an entirely different church body. God hates division. In 1 Corinthians 11:18-26, Apostle Paul rebuked the Church of Corinth with this letter: "For, in the first place, when you come together as a church, I hear that there are divisions among you. And I believe it in part, for there must be factions among you in order that those who are genuine among you may be recognized. When you come together, it is not the Lord's supper that you eat. For in eating, each one goes ahead with his own meal. One goes hungry, another gets drunk. What! Do you not have houses to eat and drink in? Or do you despise the church of God and humiliate those who have nothing? What shall I say to you? Shall I commend you in this? No, I will not. For I received from the Lord what I also delivered to you, that the Lord Jesus on the night when he was betrayed took bread, and when he had given thanks, he broke it, and said, 'This is my body, which is for you. Do this in remembrance of me.' In the same way also he took the cup, after supper, saying, 'This cup is the new covenant in my blood. Do this, as often as you drink it, in remembrance of me.' For as often as you eat this bread and drink the cup, you proclaim the Lord's death until he comes." In the Church of Corinth, people were dishonoring the Lord's communion. They weren't sitting at the table together; some of the partakers were eating too much bread, while others were drinking too much wine. It simply became a party where certain people were being honored and fed, all the while, others were not allowed to partake of the bread and the wine because they were considered nobodies. Anytime you see false prophets, you will see divisions because false prophets will always honor the people who have the most money and the most power. They will seat such a people in the best seats and completely disregard anyone they feel is of no benefit to themselves.

Envy: Envy is like its evil cousin, jealousy, but the difference between the two is their trajectory. A jealous person covets what another person has, but an envious person covets who another person is. A false prophet will, for example, attack any big name celebrity, not because he or she sees error in the celebrity; they attack the identities that they want to steal.

Drunkenness: Of course, we know that drunkenness simply means to be intoxicated, but what many don't realize is alcohol is not the only tool that we can use to get drunk. To be drunk, biblically speaking, simply means to be bewitched or overtaken by a foreign set of beliefs that contradict the Word of God. For example, a man or woman can be intoxicated by false doctrine or drunk with power. To be sober-minded means to have a sober, stable mind and a solid set of beliefs. 1 Peter 5:8 warns us this way, "Be sober, be vigilant; because your adversary the devil, as a roaring lion, walketh about, seeking whom he may devour." Simply put, you need to be alert and watchful. A false prophet is a power-thirsty, money addict who will do or say just about anything to get the gods in which he or she truly worships.

Orgies: Google defines "orgy" this way: "A wild party, especially one involving excessive drinking and unrestrained sexual activity." You have to remember that false prophets do not have their flesh under control, and for this reason, they are led by their flesh. Galatians 5:19-21 tells us what to look for in regards to non-submitted, out of control flesh. It reads, "Now the works of the flesh are evident: sexual immorality, impurity, sensuality, idolatry, sorcery, enmity, strife, jealousy, fits of anger, rivalries, dissensions, divisions, envy, drunkenness, orgies, and things like these. I warn you, as I warned you before, that those who do such things will not inherit the kingdom of God" (ESV). However, true prophets of God are led by the Spirit of God, and the fruit of the Spirit are listed 5:22-23. It reads, "But the fruit of the Spirit is love, joy, peace, patience, kindness, goodness, faithfulness, gentleness, self-control; against such things there is no law" (ESV).

To know the difference between a false prophet and a true prophet is to simply know how to identify the fruit of the flesh versus the fruit of the Spirit. If you see a person who claims to be a prophet of the Lord, and yet, that person does not have his or her flesh under control, you are looking at a false prophet. Proverbs 25:28 reads, "He that hath no rule over his own spirit is like a city that is broken down, and without walls."

It goes without saying that a lot of what we call church hurt is the direct result of God's sheep coming in contact with false prophets. This is why we have to learn to identify fruit. We shouldn't be so desperate to receive a prophetic word that we end up chasing everyone who claims to have a word from the Lord.

A Look at Trauma

Have you ever had someone to hear something you said and take it way out of perspective? Have you ever done something you thought was a good thing, only to have someone take offense and misinterpret your intentions? I think we have all experienced this, but the reality is most leaders experience this weekly, if not daily. The truth is — when dealing with human beings, you are almost always gambling because you don't know how they will respond. You won't always know if a person has been traumatized at some point, therefore, you won't always say the right thing, do the right thing or move in the right timing. As a human being, you are always going to be wrong in someone's eyes, regardless of what you do and how you do it. This is important for us to consider because as I mentioned earlier, not all church hurt stems from faulty leadership. Some church hurt is nothing but the direct result of ungodly expectations, unresolved trauma, and suspicion. For example, as a leader, I'm careful with how I approach women. I can't hug every woman or perform what I may feel to be harmless gestures like placing my hand on their shoulders. The reason for this is — some women have been molested, raped or sexually assaulted by men, and if they are not completely healed, such gestures could scare or scar them. This is why in a lot of churches, male leaders will ask the female members of their helps ministry team to lay hands on the women they want to pray for, to catch any woman who falls down after being prayed for, and to cover any woman who's fallen down under the power of God. We live in a time where a lot of people have been severely traumatized, and for this reason, we all have to be careful.

Every person has a personality and one's personality is simply the fingerprint of his or her character. It is the identifying marks of an individual; the expressive language of the heart. It lets us know where they are in Christ Jesus and it helps us to identify them by their words, works and strongholds. Trauma leaves impressions on our personalities. Think of it this way: we all have our own unique fingerprints; no one in this entire world has our fingerprints. As a matter of fact, our

A Look at Trauma

fingerprints took form in our mothers' wombs. Anyhow, our fingerprints will return after our fingers have sustained most traumas, however, if our dermis has been damaged in any way, the fingerprint may not return. Google defines the word "dermis" this way: "The thick layer of living tissue below the epidermis that forms the true skin, containing blood capillaries, nerve endings, sweat glands, hair follicles, and other structures."

If, for example, I were to cut my finger down to the dermis layer, my fingerprint would be somewhat altered because the trauma was deep. Additionally, second and third degree burns are powerful enough to remove fingerprints. You can get a second degree burn in the kitchen and that could place a scar where a part of your fingerprint once was. The same goes for the human personality.

All of our personalities have been formed by God, but they were deformed by sin, hurt and trauma. This is why God says that we have to be transformed by the renewing of our minds. In other words, God has to reform us all over again. If reformation does not take place, we tend to be led by our past hurts, traumas and the belief systems that were established in those hurts and traumas — and this only leads to more pain. For example, if a man was mistreated by his mother his entire life, his personality was deformed by that trauma. Sure, we would see facets of who he is, but we would also witness what he became as a result of that trauma. If that man were to get married before he received full healing, deliverance and understanding, he would, by default, mistreat his wife. Why is this? It's simple. Whenever we've been traumatized, we start grouping people together and creating mental labels for them. For example, a woman who keeps getting cheated on in relationships may find herself saying that all men cheat, when this is not true. Because of the trauma she has experienced, she will group all men together. We do this as human beings to help simplify our lives, meaning, by saying that all men cheat, she does not take responsibility for her own wrongs. She happens to be attracted to the wrong types of men, but rather than confront the condition of her own heart, it is easier for her to say that all men cheat. This allows her to continue to date the same type of men, all the while, justifying their behavior and developing strategies to protect herself from being cheated on or she'll learn to tolerate cheating men. One of the ways she'll learn to tolerate cheaters is by absolving them of their deeds and placing the blame on the women they cheated with. Another example is — someone who's been hurt by the church may group all believers together and begin to label them as "church folks." This allows them to justify not going to church and to verbally attack anyone who dares to say the name of Jesus. By doing this, they absolve themselves of the responsibility to forgive because, let's be honest with ourselves, it is easier to stay in the states of mind that we're currently in than it is for us to take the necessary steps toward change. All the same, a man who has been hurt by his mother may mentally create a category called "all women" and he'll file his mother's negative behaviors into that category. Let's say that in this category, there are hundreds of items on his list, including: All women are: (naggers, cheaters, liars, evil). Anytime his wife does anything or appears to be doing anything that reminds him of his mother, he will find himself saying, "All you women are the same!" From there, he'll spew a bunch of ungodly rhetoric that he came to believe while under the care of his mother. And because he's broken, he has the tendency to attract broken women, thus, causing his self-evolved theories to seem right in his eyes.

Most, if not all, leaders have experienced some form of trauma, just as most, if not all, non-leaders have experienced some level of trauma. However, when that trauma is deep, it has taken an effect on their personalities and caused them to become snippets of who they once were. Again, this is why we have to be transformed by the renewing of our minds.

Trauma is nothing but the impressions on our personalities' fingerprints; it is our own personal stripes that we've acquired through life. When a leader has been traumatized deeply, you will see that trauma in the leader's personality, hear it in his/ her words or witness it in the leader's choices. This is, of course, if the leader has not gone through the proper healing process. A lot of church hurt is the result of traumatized leaders responding to others through their trauma. The truth is that some leaders are good men and women who've been traumatized by the sheep they were once entrusted

A Look at Trauma

to lead. It is not uncommon to hear stories about leaders who've invested five or more years into developing a person and even taken time out from their busy schedules to help that particular person, only to have that person walk away without so much as a goodbye. Believe it or not, this can be traumatic for a leader who loves the people he or she has been shepherding. You see, when it comes to us leaders, most folks expect us to bounce back quickly and just keep on preaching. This leads to a phenomena that most call "leading while bleeding." Needless to say, we are human and because we are human, any wound that is not properly dealt with can easily become a traumatic fingerprint on our character. And when these traumas aren't dealt with, we develop negative characteristics to counter, respond to and protect ourselves from trauma. Now, this does not justify a leader mishandling the sheep; my goal is to explain it so that you'll know how to pray.

Something else we need to visit is congregational trauma. Let me explain it this way: hurt people not only hurt people, but they attract others who are hurt. So, let's say that Todd starts a new church in his living room. Todd is a loving, nurturing, no-nonsense type of leader who tends to be very protective of the people he covers. Because of his fatherly-like personality, Todd is going to attract a lot of hurting people to himself, and this isn't a bad thing, after all, Jesus came to set the captives free. Todd will attract men who didn't have a father-figure growing up, women who have been hurt by men and young men and women who want to experience disciplinary love. For this reason, Todd needs to be very prayerful about how he leads the people who've joined his church. If he does not, what's going to happen is — the congregation will lead him. Let's get this straight — the congregation is looking to Todd because they have needs and they have been led astray by those needs for years. Todd's job is to get them to depend on Jesus, but if he does not take and maintain authority, he will be led by the needs of the people, meaning, no one will get healed. Instead, the members of Todd's church will be coddled. Eventually, Todd's home is going to start overflowing with hurting people who have no desire to change — people who are looking to Todd to fix their lives. Todd will have to find a church building and his church will start to pack out quickly, but this isn't a good thing because no one is getting helped. Everyone is simply casting their problems on Todd.

Because the people aren't changing, those strongholds in their lives and those ungodly mindsets aren't being confronted. So, many of the people who once came to Todd's church looking for answers, a father-figure, and love will find themselves getting hurt by other members. The reason for this is that everyone there is still walking in their Adam-nature, meaning, they have not been changed by the renewing of their minds. This explains much of the church hurt we hear about coming from certain church bodies. Anytime people are coddled but not taught, they will flock to the person or people who's coddling them. From there, they will proceed to wear out and even kill that person, in addition to hurting one another. One of the roles of parents is to discipline the children they have. Discipline is one of the facets of love. If Todd had loved his members enough to discipline them, his church may not have packed out as fast, but he would have received people who wanted to change, versus people who are looking for an excuse to stay as they are. Unbeknownst to him, Todd has created a gang where he is the leader; it's no different than a street gang, only the members gather inside of a church building and have bible study. Anytime a leader places quantity over quality, that leader will create an atmosphere where hurting people will hurt and further traumatize one another. In other words, that leader will essentially become the leader of a gang and not a true body of believers.

It goes without saying that the congregants aren't the only people who experience church hurt; many people in leadership experience this hurt from other leaders. Of course, everyone responds to pain differently. Responding to church hurt is a sensitive matter, especially when you're a leader and the person who's hurt you is also a leader. Obviously, the correct response is to pray for the person who's hurt you, but let's be honest with ourselves. It's not always easy to behave like a Christian when the person who's hurt us also identifies himself or herself as a Christian. The reason for this is — we expect them to know better. What can you say to someone who probably knows more scripture than you do? How do you correct the incorrigible?

A Look at Trauma

A young man is approached by some of the members of his church's deacon board. They told him that he displayed the conduct and dress of a deacon. After this, they asked him to join the board. The young man expressed that he did not know what a deacon was required to do, but he was willing to be trained as a deacon. After being trained for a few months, a problem arose in the church and people started taking sides. The young man mentioned it to the other deacons, concerned about a split in the church. The deacons told him to just agree when they agree. They said to him, "When the vote comes, you stand when you see us stand." But the young man did not agree with the other deacons and told them he would not feel comfortable standing with them. The deacons verbally attacked the young man and told him he would no longer be trained as a deacon in their church. Confused about his free will being challenged as a Christian, he left that church and never accepted any position offered to him in other churches he joined.

This is a classic case of church hurt. Even more than that, this is a case of church trauma. Hurt and trauma are similar, but the difference between the two are the impact they have on the individual. For example, a child can fall down and hurt himself, but this hurt wasn't necessarily traumatic. It didn't leave any scarring, nor will it cause the child to be afraid to walk again. However, that same child can fall off a bicycle and scar both of his knees. Because the fall, in itself, was terrifying, plus, some of his skin was broken, that child may experience psychological trauma that leads to fear. To get him to get back on the bicycle and try to peddle again won't be an easy job because the scarring on his knees will serve as a painful reminder to him that he can lose control while on the bicycle.

Trauma can be physical, psychological and spiritual. For example, the scars on the young man's knees are called physical trauma, meaning, the fall made a lasting impression on his skin. Psychological trauma is basically horrific memories. This happens when a traumatic incident scars a person's perception, beliefs and life altogether. Falling on the bicycle is a good example of psychological trauma, but of course, it can be far deeper than that. A person who suffered through sexual abuse as a

A Look at Trauma

child, for example, would suffer through deep-rooted psychological trauma. Spiritual trauma is extremely deep-rooted psychological trauma that has not only affected a person's perception of this life, but of the life to come. Proverbs 18:14 reads, "The spirit of a man can endure his sickness, but as for a broken spirit who can bear it?" (NASB).

The point is — there are different levels of trauma. Church hurt can be psychological or it can be spiritual. Some people have turned away from the faith because of deep-rooted church hurt. Sure, neither you nor I can understand why anyone would let another person or group of people drive them away from the faith, but the reality is — not everyone has the same measure of faith. Romans 12:3 reads, "For by the grace given to me I say to everyone among you not to think of himself more highly than he ought to think, but to think with sober judgment, each according to the measure of faith that God has assigned" (ESV). What this should tell us is that it is not wise for us to judge people who have strayed or turned from the faith because of church hurt or church trauma. Instead, our assignment is to bring them to the healer Himself.

Our assignment is to love them, pray for them and display the true love of God to them.

Drive Them to Their Needs

Everywhere you go in life, you are going to come in contact with people who can best be described as unloving, and therefore, unlovable souls. They may be loud, unforgiving, presumptuous, controlling, easily offended and legalistic. In other words, you will come in contact with plenty of people who are not a joy to be around. Because of their ways, you will find that a lot of people who are like this don't have strong family connections because their natural families will often avoid them because of how obnoxious they appear to be. For this reason, they will always go looking for people they can call their own self-made families. And guess what? Sometimes, they conduct their searches in church. What are you to do when you find yourself seated next to a talkative, overbearing soul who won't let you get a word in? Even worse, what should you do when that person, after sitting next to you one Sunday, suddenly feels the need to sit next to you every Sunday? The answer is simple: you love the soul, often reminding yourself that God created and loves that soul as well.

There is a language of love that most believers are completely unaware of. Love is one language, but it has many dialects and cultural expressions. For this reason, we, as believers, tend to create cliques in the church. Cliques are nothing but comfort zones; they are an expressive form of monolingualism in the love arena. A monolingual is a person who can only speak one language. Consider what God did when He confused the languages of the people in Genesis 11:6. This is when He confused the languages of the people to stop them from building the Tower of Babel. Here's an interesting truth: when God confused the peoples' languages, this did not make building the Tower impossible; it simply meant that they would have had to tap in to a level of love that, quite frankly, they did not understand. They would have had to learn to work together, despite their differences. Needless to say, God knew that confusing their language would be enough to get them to stop building. God didn't do this to hurt His people; the truth was that they were simply trying to illegally access Heaven.

Satan also understands the power of confusion. As a matter of fact, confusion and discord are two of his favorite weapons. You see, if you place a monolingual believer next to an unbeliever that the believer does not understand, what you'll witness is the unbeliever behaving in a more loving way than the believer. This is because unbelievers, in their attempts to survive and flourish, tend to be more open to people they do not understand than cliquish believers. Of course, this is something that we, as a church, must address.

1 John 4:20 says, "If anyone says, "I love God," and hates his brother, he is a liar; for he who does not love his brother whom he has seen cannot love God whom he has not seen" (ESV). Of course, most believers will never admit to hating another believer. Let's take it a step further. What I've found is that most believers who are slaves to hatred don't even realize that they are bound. I love a famous quote by Harriet Tubman that reads, "I freed a thousand slaves. I could have freed a thousand more if only they knew they were slaves." This is still true today. There are believers who hate other believers and unbelievers, but they are blind to this

truth and deaf to correction.

In 2011, aerial photographers in Peru captured a photograph of what they called an uncontacted Amazon tribe. Now dubbed the Moxihatetema tribe, the group lives off the land and had never had any contact with the outside world. The Amazon Rainforest that they are living in stretches across South America for 2.1 million square miles and it connects Brazil to Peru.

Why hadn't the Moxihatetema people ever had any contact with others? After all, there are other tribes in the forest, but most of those tribes have made contact with the outside world. The answer is simple: they likely wanted no contact with the outside world. Their tribe was their own unique world and they were comfortable enough to remain unconnected. This sounds like a good idea considering contact with the outside world could mean opening themselves up for diseases that they have no resistance against. It also could mean genocide. There are many possibilities, and most of us can understand why they don't want to be connected to the outside world. However, being unconnected is never a good idea. Why not?

Recently, that same tribe found themselves running for their lives after they came in contact with loggers. A logger is a lumberjack or basically, a person who chops down trees and harvests lumber. Afraid for their lives, they ran to the Brazil-Peruvian border where they came in contact with a group of people called the Asháninka Indians. At first, they were afraid to approach the Asháninkans, but eventually, their needs drove them to make contact. In the beginning, they started stealing pots and food, but eventually, they made contact and the contact has remained peaceful. What they soon found was that they needed their neighbors. There is strength in numbers. Sure, there are always risks when dealing with people, but risks are just a part of life. Every time we turn on our stoves, we risk our homes catching on fire. Every time we crank up our cars, we risk having a car accident. Every time we breathe in and out, we risk inhaling something that could potentially be fatal. The point is — if we didn't take risks in life, we'd all be dead or crazy. We can't live our lives worrying about the "what if's." Instead, we simply need to trust God.

The Moxihatetema eventually returned to what they

knew. They went back off on their own and weren't seen for an entire year. They were presumed to be dead until they were discovered in a new location. Of course, they weren't happy being photographed, but the truth is — the risks that they are taking by remaining unconnected is greater than the risks they would be taking if they connected to, at minimum, their neighbors. How so? Illegal miners are known to peruse the Amazon forest in search of gold and some of those guys are blood-thirsty. The Moxihatetema tribe arms themselves with spears, but spears are pretty much ineffective against men with guns. So, what will have to happen yet again is that the tribe will eventually be driven to contact other tribes (at minimum) when they find themselves in need.

In the biblical days, it was common for two or more nations to link up so that they could protect themselves from opposing nations. They understood the strength in not just numbers, but the strength that comes through connecting with people you simply do not understand. After all, they have a different perspective, which would also lead them to having a different strategy in the arena of

Drive Them to Their Needs

warfare. If only church folks understood this today.

It goes without saying that the enemy keeps us divided because he fears corporate prayer and corporate unity. His favorite weapon is called "lack of knowledge." You see, monolingual believers are just like the Moxihatetema people. They prefer to congregate with people who are like themselves — people they feel comfortable around. This prison, also referred to as a comfort zone, is nothing but the perimeters or limitations of a person's love. Our love for one another is measured by our love of God and our understanding of what love is. A person who is not versed in the many dialects of love will find himself or herself having limited dealings in life. This limits that person's growth, finances and capacity. Needless to say, however, cliquish believers are often driven outside their comfort zones when the people in their comfort zones are unable to help them to meet certain needs. God designed it this way so that we would not be able to flourish much outside of one another. Remember, He is not just a God of love, but 1 John 4:8 tells us that He is love.

Drive Them to Their Needs

What's the point of this chapter? I want to give you something to consider. Now, this may or may not apply to you, but it does apply to many believers who have suffered through what we collectively refer to as "church hurt." What I've come to learn is that some church hurt is simply God's way of breaking up cliques. It's simply God's way of driving people out of their comfort zones, whether that comfort zone be in a clique, a certain church or wherever it may be. Some people who say they were hurt by the church were simply hurt by the people they once congregated around. This isn't necessarily church hurt. More often than not, it is simply a case of God confusing the language of a group of people so they can stop building whatever it is that they're building. We all know that gossip tends to flourish in cliques, and just as we know this, God knows this.

Another common complaint is — many people say they left their church because after, for example, they'd gotten sick, they were disappointed to see that they had not been contacted by their pastors or anyone in their local church bodies. This offense is not always justifiable, considering that some

Drive Them to Their Needs

churches are so big that it would take an incredible amount of resources and time for them to not only contact, but keep in contact with their ailing members. Of course, every church should try to find a workaround so that they can know what's going on with the sick and shut-in, but the truth is, just like people, churches go through transitions. Some churches get caught up in a growth spurt and it is during that time that they offend the most members, but not intentionally. Oftentimes, the problem is — they are coming in contact with problems they didn't initially have. Then again, some people will not let you know that they are sick. They literally expect you to notice their absences and reach out to them, and again, this isn't always an easy task. After all, it adds to the already strenuous task of running a church. Of course, some churches are small and the leaders don't reach out to their absent members because the members are absent quite often or the leaders simply didn't notice their absences. Whatever the issue may be, becoming angry with a leader or a group of believers for not contacting you when you were away can sometimes be unfair to that body. And sometimes, what God is doing is getting you to look outside of the church that you've chosen for yourself so that He can lead you to the body of believers that He has chosen for you. However, you have to be willing to grow with the church. One of the biggest hindrances to small churches are members who are adamant about keeping them small. This selfish behavior stunts and closes church, in addition to keeping so many locals from hearing the gospel of Jesus Christ.

Researchers say that people who travel tend to be more successful than people who don't. This is especially true for people who travel abroad. There are several reasons for this, including:
1. Traveling the world makes you more sensitive and loving towards others who are unlike you — we tend to be insensitive and unloving towards anything we do not understand, including people. When we travel, we are no longer relying on textbooks and news reports to tell us about certain countries; we get a firsthand view of those countries and we are able to develop our own opinions in regards to them. People who've never traveled outside their countries

tend to be less loving towards foreigners and more prideful in regards to dealing with foreigners because they've never experienced what it is like to be a foreigner.
2. Traveling the world brings you outside of your comfort zone — Comfort zones can serve as beautifully decorated prisons that we happily sentence ourselves to. What you'll learn in life is the more you take yourself out of your comfort zone, the more risks you'll take in life. People who take risks are more likely to be successful than people who don't.
3. Traveling the world strengthens your faith in God — Most believers who travel tend to pray more. They pray for traveling mercy and they tend to pray for the people they meet abroad. Having an increased prayer life often leads to increased faith. Additionally, if you ever visit a country where Christianity is not the dominant religion, you will better understand the need for Christ.
4. Traveling allows you to expand your network — It goes without saying that when you travel, there are endless opportunities to make potentially beneficial connections for

your business, ministry or your own personal life.
5. Traveling changes your perspective on life and people as a whole — Gossip and slander are honestly most common in small towns, among people who have never traveled. They talk about others because they've run out of other stuff to talk about. However, a person who travels tends to see the bigger picture that is life. For this reason, travelers tend to have a more positive outlook on life than people who've never traveled.

Apply this information to your relationships, especially within your local church body. People who are not bound by cliquish mindsets tend to be more successful and more loving, whereas, cliquish souls tend to be more judgmental, pompous and self-righteous. When believers avoid other believers simply because they do not understand them, they do themselves a great injustice. They keep themselves from experiencing some potentially great, healthy and lifelong friendships and from getting some of their life's needs met.

I believe that God intentionally places what we need, during any given season, in the hands of people we simply do not relate to. This forces us to put away our differences and learn to love what we do not understand. This forces us to become multilingual in the love arena, thus, allowing God to promote and enrich us all the more. Sometimes, the answer to your prayers is locked away in the heart of a person you are not interested in knowing. Your apprehension about knowing that person has everything to do with your fear and lack of knowledge in regards to the unknown. This is why we experience storms in our lives. Sometimes, storms are nothing but winds that have come to blow us out of our comfort zones. Sure, when these winds hit us in church, we may all refer to it as church hurt, but further prayer and examination would expose it for what it really is: a disrupted comfort zone. Sometimes, it's nothing but God driving us out of our tribal mindsets so that He can take us global.

A New Perspective

Let's get one thing out of the way: Jesus dealt with church hurt. John 1:9-13 reads, "The true light, which gives light to everyone, was coming into the world. He was in the world, and the world was made through him, yet the world did not know him. He came to his own, and his own people did not receive him. But to all who did receive him, who believed in his name, he gave the right to become children of God, who were born, not of blood nor of the will of the flesh nor of the will of man, but of God" (ESV). Isaiah 53:3 reads, "He was despised and rejected by men, a man of sorrows and acquainted with grief; and as one from whom men hide their faces he was despised, and we esteemed him not."

Jesus had to deal with a lot of hurt and rejection during his earthly ministry. This wasn't because of anything wrong He'd done. It had everything to do with the people being legalistic and religious. To be religious means to conform to the letter of the law with no understanding of God's heart. It means to create laws and cultures based on your understanding of the bible or your religion's understanding of the bible. Jesus lived in a time when the Pharisees and the Sadducees were considered by the Israelites to be their teachers. The Pharisees and the Sadducees were legalistic and religious, and even though they criticized and judged people for not being able to uphold the law, they themselves could not uphold the law. They were hypocrites who turned religion into a profitable business and a who's who in regards to power and money. When Jesus came along, He interfered with the systems that they'd put in place — systems they'd mastered and profited from. For this reason, not only did they reject Him, but they encouraged their followers to reject Him as well.

The rejection Jesus suffered was not limited to His peers; He also experienced rejection from the people He'd grown up around. Mark 6:1-6 reads, "He went away from there and came to his hometown, and his disciples followed him. And on the Sabbath he began to teach in the synagogue, and many who heard him were astonished, saying, "Where did this man get these things? What is the wisdom given to him? How are such mighty works done by his hands? Is not this the carpenter, the son of Mary and brother of James and Joses and Judas and Simon? And are not his sisters here with us?" And they took offense at him. And Jesus said to them, "A prophet is not without honor, except in his hometown and among his relatives and in his own household." And he could do no mighty work there, except that he laid his hands on a few sick people and healed them. And he marveled because of their unbelief" (ESV).

In the end, it was the people closest to Him who'd deserted Him. Desertion can be short-term or permanent rejection. Mark 14:43-50 reads, "And immediately, while he was still speaking, Judas came, one of the twelve, and with him a crowd with swords and clubs, from the chief priests and the scribes and the elders. Now the betrayer had given them a sign, saying, "The one I will kiss is the man. Seize him and lead him away under guard." And when he came, he went up to him at once and said, "Rabbi!" And he kissed him. And they laid hands on him and seized him. But one of those who stood by drew his sword and struck the servant of the high priest and cut off his ear. And Jesus said to them, "Have you come out as against a robber, with swords and clubs to capture me? Day after day I was with you in the temple teaching, and you did not seize me. But let the Scriptures be fulfilled." And they all left him and fled" (ESV).

Jesus was persecuted, deserted, betrayed and killed. Peter denied Him three times and Judas, of course, betrayed Him. As we can see, the Lord experienced a lot of rejection, and not just from people afar off, but from the people closest to Him. This tells us that we are to expect to be rejected, persecuted and deserted. Matthew 5:10 prepares us with these words, "Blessed are those who have been persecuted for the sake of righteousness, for theirs is the kingdom of heaven" (NASB). Matthew 24: 9 goes on to say, "Then they will deliver you up to tribulation and put you to death, and you will be hated by all nations for my name's sake" (ESV). In other words, if we are teaching and demonstrating the true gospel of Jesus Christ, we should expect to be persecuted. This means that a large number of people who have experienced being wounded in the church have a reason to celebrate. Anytime we

A New Perspective

suffer for His name's sake, we store up for ourselves rewards in heaven.

One of my favorite stories takes place in the book of Acts. "Now many signs and wonders were regularly done among the people by the hands of the apostles. And they were all together in Solomon's Portico. None of the rest dared join them, but the people held them in high esteem. And more than ever believers were added to the Lord, multitudes of both men and women, so that they even carried out the sick into the streets and laid them on cots and mats, that as Peter came by at least his shadow might fall on some of them. The people also gathered from the towns around Jerusalem, bringing the sick and those afflicted with unclean spirits, and they were all healed.
But the high priest rose up, and all who were with him (that is, the party of the Sadducees), and filled with jealousy they arrested the apostles and put them in the public prison. But during the night an angel of the Lord opened the prison doors and brought them out, and said, 'Go and stand in the temple and speak to the people all the words of this Life.' And when they heard this, they entered the

223

temple at daybreak and began to teach. Now when the high priest came, and those who were with him, they called together the council, all the senate of the people of Israel, and sent to the prison to have them brought. But when the officers came, they did not find them in the prison, so they returned and reported, 'We found the prison securely locked and the guards standing at the doors, but when we opened them we found no one inside.' Now when the captain of the temple and the chief priests heard these words, they were greatly perplexed about them, wondering what this would come to. And someone came and told them, 'Look! The men whom you put in prison are standing in the temple and teaching the people.' Then the captain with the officers went and brought them, but not by force, for they were afraid of being stoned by the people. And when they had brought them, they set them before the council. And the high priest questioned them, saying, 'We strictly charged you not to teach in this name, yet here you have filled Jerusalem with your teaching, and you intend to bring this man's blood upon us.' But Peter and the apostles answered, 'We must obey God rather than men. The God of our fathers raised Jesus,

A New Perspective

whom you killed by hanging him on a tree. God exalted him at his right hand as Leader and Savior, to give repentance to Israel and forgiveness of sins. And we are witnesses to these things, and so is the Holy Spirit, whom God has given to those who obey him.' When they heard this, they were enraged and wanted to kill them. But a Pharisee in the council named Gamaliel, a teacher of the law held in honor by all the people, stood up and gave orders to put the men outside for a little while. And he said to them, 'Men of Israel, take care what you are about to do with these men. For before these days Theudas rose up, claiming to be somebody, and a number of men, about four hundred, joined him. He was killed, and all who followed him were dispersed and came to nothing. After him Judas the Galilean rose up in the days of the census and drew away some of the people after him. He too perished, and all who followed him were scattered. So in the present case I tell you, keep away from these men and let them alone, for if this plan or this undertaking is of man, it will fail; but if it is of God, you will not be able to overthrow them. You might even be found opposing God!' So they took his advice, and when they had called in the apostles, they beat them and charged them not to speak in the name of Jesus, and let them go. Then they left the presence of the council, rejoicing that they were counted worthy to suffer dishonor for the name. And every day, in the temple and from house to house, they did not cease teaching and preaching that the Christ is Jesus."

The apostles were suffering one of the highest levels of persecution. Their accusers were filled with jealousy towards them and because of this, they wanted to have them killed. Despite the accusations, persecutions and the threats, the apostles kept on teaching and healing others. They were then beat and told to not speak in the name of Jesus Christ anymore, and instead of crying church hurt or running away from God altogether, they chose to see their sufferings for what they really were: they were suffering for His name's sake and this was and is an honor. Sadly enough, we don't see persecution this way these days. Instead, we allow a simple offense to drive us away from the church altogether. This is because we have been coddled for far too long. We don't know how to endure simple sufferings. Could you imagine the great falling away that would take place if the Antichrist was in the earth now, killing Christians? This isn't to minimize anyone's experience; it is to say that we have got to develop tougher skin and stop allowing gossip, rumors, slander and blackballing to cripple our walks in Christ Jesus. We should, instead, be rejoicing for suffering for His name's sake.

What we have to do as a church is change our perspective in regards to persecution, rejection, betrayal, desertion and the like. Sure, none of it feels good, but it's just the price we pay for loving our God and He is not only worthy of our praise, but He is worthy of our pain. He suffered for us; far be it from us that we are not willing to suffer for Him. We have to take on the apostles' perspectives to ensure that we run this race all the way to the finish line. If we allow hurt and offense to drive us into unforgiveness, bitterness or isolation, we have allowed the enemy's darts to effectively penetrate us. Instead, we should do like the apostles and keep on preaching, teaching and living for the Lord. I can't tell you how many believers who have "fainted" because of offense. To "faint" means to lose consciousness. In other biblical translations, outside of the King James Bible, it is translated to mean "to give up." In other words, a person who faints is intentionally unaware of the devil's schemes. Why intentionally? Because every incident that arises has a root and we can search it out if we so choose. Some people choose not to pray or search out a matter because they are too busy mulling over what was done or said to them. This demonic distraction only causes them to highlight their offenses, instead of extracting the wisdom from them. Galatians 6:9 says, "And let us not grow weary of doing good, for in due season we will reap, if we do not give up" (ESV).

Reviewing and complaining about offenses only causes us to relive the incidents that wounded us. It goes without saying that this keeps us from receiving the healing we'll need to move forward. I decided long ago to take my story and do something awesome with it. Instead of complaining about the people who tried to stop me, I decided to focus on the God who wouldn't allow them to stop me. Do you see how a change in perspective can keep you from becoming bitter and giving up? I smile because I have a testimony to share. I smile because

A New Perspective

people have placed stop signs in front of my assignment, but through the grace of God, I've run them all. Change your perspective about whatever it was that was done to you. Rejoice for being counted worthy to suffer for His name's sake, even if you weren't completely in right-standing with Him. Remember this: sometimes, the devil doesn't attack us because of where we are; he attacks us because of where we're going. It's up to us, however, if we allow him to stop us from getting there.

Understanding Measures

God is a God of measure, meaning, He measures everything. A few scriptures to look are:
Matthew 7:2 (ESV): For with the judgment you pronounce you will be judged, and with the measure you use it will be measured to you.
Luke 6:37-38 (ESV): Judge not, and you will not be judged; condemn not, and you will not be condemned; forgive, and you will be forgiven; give, and it will be given to you. Good measure, pressed down, shaken together, running over, will be put into your lap. For with the measure you use it will be measured back to you."
Proverbs 1:11 (ESV): A false balance is an abomination to the LORD, but a just weight is his delight.
Proverbs 20:10 (ESV): Unequal weights and unequal measures are both alike an abomination to the LORD.
Proverbs 16:11 (ESV): A just balance and scales are the LORD's; all the weights in the bag are his work.
Ezekiel 45:9 (ESV): Thus says the Lord GOD:

Enough, O princes of Israel! Put away violence and oppression, and execute justice and righteousness. Cease your evictions of my people, declares the Lord GOD.

Notice that God considers the words "just" and "balance" to be synonymous with the word "measure." Additionally, the word "just" is a short form of the word "justice." So, as we can see, God is a God of balance, order and justice. He is the Righteous Judge, and for this reason, He warns us in the book of Luke to do unto others as we would have them to do unto us. He says it this way in Luke 6:27-31, "But I say to you who hear, Love your enemies, do good to those who hate you, bless those who curse you, pray for those who abuse you. To one who strikes you on the cheek, offer the other also, and from one who takes away your cloak do not withhold your tunic either. Give to everyone who begs from you, and from one who takes away your goods do not demand them back. And as you wish that others would do to you, do so to them" (ESV).

The reason God told us to love our enemies and

pretty much let them do whatever evil they think is necessary to us is because whatever we do to others, God measures back to us. In other words, if a man walked up to me and struck me on my face, that man has just incurred the wrath of God. However, if I return to him what he has given me and I strike him back, God now has to respond to my choice. He now has to measure back to me what I did to that man. This doesn't mean that He will send another man to strike me. What it means is that I've sown a seed and I will reap whatsoever I sow. If I want to provoke God to bless me, I have to use that moment to do something godly. In that moment, if that man wants to take my coat, the bible tells me to give it to him. If he's cursing me, my assignment is to bless him. By doing so, I set myself up for a blessing, but if I allow my flesh to rise up and provoke me to wrath, I set myself up for a fall. Proverbs 16:18 warns us this way, "Pride goes before destruction, and a haughty spirit before a fall" (ESV). This means that in this moment, I have to intentionally humble myself; in this moment, my fear of God has got to be greater than my desire to avenge myself. Now, I'm not saying that if some strange guy walks up and starts attacking you that

Understanding Measures

you should lie there. In some cases, you have to defend yourself and your family, but there are those cases where, for example, people who are offended with you may make a decision to touch you with their hands or their mouths. When this happens, you need to remember that God is a God of measure. You measure out to that person what you want God to measure back out to you.

With that being said, we have to understand that much of what we call "church hurt" is us receiving our measure — we are receiving what we've dished out to others, even if what we've sown was sown outside of the church. For example, let's say that a woman named Elizabeth has been very cruel to her sister, Anna. Elizabeth is a Christian; her sister is not, but the two women have a very active and contentious relationship.

Elizabeth feels that her verbal lashings of Anna are justified since her sister isn't saved. Additionally, Elizabeth spends quite a bit of her time talking to other believers about Anna's ways. "She's always at the club getting drunk and doing God knows what!" Elizabeth says to one of her closest friends about

Anna. "And then, my mother called me and told me that Anna is pregnant again! I can guarantee you she doesn't know who the father of that baby is!" Elizabeth, in her own self-righteousness, thinks that her words prove her love for and loyalty to God, but this isn't true. Instead, Elizabeth is not acting in love; she is being a judgmental gossip, whose ways may very much be driving Anna further and further away from God.

One day, Elizabeth hears a rumor about herself. One of the women she's been gossiping to is now gossiping about her. That woman has told a few people at their church that Elizabeth is in a relationship with a guy who barely calls her — a guy who's clearly not interested in her. The woman has also told a few people that Elizabeth is mean-spirited and treats her sister poorly. Now, all of these things are true, but they are hurtful to Elizabeth.

Offended and hurt, Elizabeth tells the pastor about the rumor mill that's spinning in regards to her. "This is supposed to be the house of the Lord," Elizabeth shouts. "I have never said anything

Understanding Measures

negative about Catherine and I would appreciate if she would keep my name out of her mouth! Please tell me what you're going to do about this!" Elizabeth's pastor apologizes to her, promising that he'll try to get to the bottom of it all. He speaks with Catherine who admits to spreading the rumors. "I wasn't trying to be mean," says Catherine. "I guess I just found her behavior so disturbing that I felt like I needed to talk to someone about it. I'll apologize to her because spreading rumors was never my intention." The pastor lovingly corrects Catherine and Catherine honors her word; she calls and apologizes to Elizabeth, but Elizabeth doesn't want to let her off so easy. "Okay. Thanks," she says before hanging up the phone.

Elizabeth feels that Catherine's offense was unforgivable because it took place in a church house, so when she sees Catherine still teaching bible study on that following Wednesday, Elizabeth finds herself enraged. She storms out of the church and immediately calls her pastor. "Pastor! I told you what that woman did to me and you still kept her as the bible study teacher! I even heard that she brought you an apple pie up to the church. Pastor, I

Understanding Measures

am officially giving you my resignation! This obviously is not the church for me because you seem to endorse messiness, instead of addressing it! Consider this my resignation, please!" To Elizabeth's surprise, the pastor simply answers with a loving, "okay." Offended and hurt, Elizabeth hangs up the phone and calls a few people to tell them about the incident. What Elizabeth does not understand is that she is experiencing measure; she is experiencing "justice."

Elizabeth justified her attack against her sister because her sister was not saved. To "justify" something simply means to determine that it is right, appropriate, and good; thus making you righteous. Howbeit, God saw injustice; He saw that the balance in Elizabeth's life was tilted in such a way that placed Elizabeth (in her mind) above her sister, Anna. This is called pride. To balance the scales, God calls us to humble ourselves, but when we do not humble ourselves, He allows us to be humbled by the very seeds we've sown. Consider, once again, the parable of the Pharisee and the Tax Collector. The story reads this way, "He also told this parable to some who trusted in themselves that

Understanding Measures

they were righteous, and treated others with contempt: "Two men went up into the temple to pray, one a Pharisee and the other a tax collector. The Pharisee, standing by himself, prayed thus: 'God, I thank you that I am not like other men, extortioners, unjust, adulterers, or even like this tax collector. I fast twice a week; I give tithes of all that I get.' But the tax collector, standing far off, would not even lift up his eyes to heaven, but beat his breast, saying, 'God, be merciful to me, a sinner!' I tell you, this man went down to his house justified, rather than the other. For everyone who exalts himself will be humbled, but the one who humbles himself will be exalted."

In this story, we witness a sinner exalting himself, all the while, criticizing others. We also witness a sinner acknowledging that he is a sinner. He humbled himself and because of this, the bible says he went away justified. What does this mean? It means that he would not reap of the sins in which he'd measured out to others. It means that God tipped the scale in his favor. It means that he was suddenly qualified to receive the undeserved favor and blessings from God. The Pharisee, however,

Understanding Measures

spoke of his works, and for this reason, he was judged by his works. James 2:10 reads, "For whoever keeps the whole law but fails in one point has become guilty of all of it" (ESV). In other words, if you're going to count your righteous deeds, you must also count the evils in which you've done. In doing so, you'd find that the Mosaic Law condemned mankind, but Jesus Christ justified us. In other words, Jesus tipped the balance in our favor.

Elizabeth eventually found herself another church home, but because she didn't know why she'd gone through what she'd gone through in the first church, she ended up experiencing the same thing in the next church. Eventually, Elizabeth left church altogether and labeled her pain as "church hurt." She joined a Christian sect that promoted a completely different gospel than the one she knew to be true and her bitterness eventually got the best of her. In Elizabeth's old age, she repented, but not before experiencing a whole lot of headaches and heartaches that came as a result of what she kept measuring out. For a long time, Elizabeth thought God was unfair and that He did not love her, but the

truth was, Elizabeth kept planting the wrong seeds and therefore, reaping a painful harvest. She hated correction and loved to be seen as a righteous servant of the Lord, when she was not. Remember God's judgment in Isaiah 29:13-14 and it reads, "And the Lord said: 'Because this people draw near with their mouth and honor me with their lips, while their hearts are far from me, and their fear of me is a commandment taught by men, therefore, behold, I will again
do wonderful things with this people,
with wonder upon wonder; and the wisdom of their wise men shall perish, and the discernment of their discerning men shall be hidden."

In Elizabeth's story, she behaved like a Pharisee. Her sister hadn't yet humbled herself, but Elizabeth did not demonstrate the love of God towards her. Instead, she criticized her and gossiped about her, but when she experienced this same behavior from someone she considered to be her sister in the Lord, she saw how hurtful it was. Again, my goal isn't to minimize what anyone has gone through; you may not be like Elizabeth. Your story may be completely different, and it is possible that you

Understanding Measures

were mishandled by your brothers and sisters in Christ. However, there are some people reading this book who are like Elizabeth and they don't know why they keep experiencing what they think of as church hurt when, in truth, they're simply reaping what they've sown. This may sound insensitive, but we don't change when we're coddled and justified in our wrongdoing; we change when we are corrected. Proverbs 12:1 says, "Whoever loves discipline loves knowledge, but whoever hates correction is stupid" (NIV). Again, this may sound cruel, but these are God's words; not mine. God doesn't speak harshly to us to condemn us; He corrects us because He loves us. Proverbs 3:11- 12 reads, "My son, do not despise the Lord's discipline or be weary of his reproof, for the Lord reproves him whom he loves, as a father the son in whom he delights." This means that we should be happy when we are corrected; it's when there is no correction that we should be concerned.

Take the time out to consider your church hurt story and ask yourself, "Have I done to others what I feel has been done to me?" Don't just consider the people in the church; consider the people outside of the church. Again, sometimes, we justify doing evil to others because in our self-righteousness, we tend to think that we are correcting them when, in truth, we are condemning them. If we want to stop the cycle of church hurt, we need to examine all angles so that we can ensure that we are not reaping something we've sown. This helps us to be self-accountable and it teaches us to be careful with the words we release towards others. Sometimes, we don't know how bad something hurts or how traumatic words can be until we receive the measure in which we've portioned out to others. This is why daily self-examination is important. It helps us to understand why we keep reaping certain harvests and being denied access to the harvests we truly want.

Healing from Church Hurt

One of the most important keys to healing from church hurt is realizing and acknowledging that you have been hurt, plus, understanding that this hurt has been affecting your life — whether you want to admit to this or not. Without admission, there can be no progress. The reason is that confession is the first part of a process; without it, the process will be in vain. 1 John 1:9 reads, "If we confess our sins, he is faithful and just and will forgive us our sins and purify us from all unrighteousness. " (NIV). Proverbs 28:13 reads, "Whoever conceals their sins does not prosper,
but the one who confesses and renounces them finds mercy" (NIV).

Of course, you're probably wondering what sin you have committed and why do you need to confess it when you're the victim. You have to confess and repent for harboring unforgiveness towards the people who hurt you. I know this doesn't seem fair, but God never tells us to do something if it wasn't beneficial for us. God told us to forgive because He knew the toll that unforgiveness would take on us if we were to walk in it. Confess your hurts, pains, and if unforgiveness is in your heart, confess it too and ask the Lord to deliver you from it.

I dealt with church hurt and I had to admit to myself that what my former leaders did actually affected me. From there, I was able to start navigating through my emotions, the questions, and every obstacle that stood in the way of my full healing. Nevertheless, I pressed through because I did not want to allow the mistakes of others to become my own. I knew that if I did not heal, I was going to repeat the mistakes of my predecessors and I did not want this to happen, so I purposely set my heart on forgiving the people who'd hurt me and understanding why they chose to do what they did. In other words, I had to go outside my perspective and try to see things from their points of view. It still didn't make sense to me, but I came to understand them a little more. This made it easier for me to move forward and move on.

Ever since I've been a leader, I've tried to maintain a

level of love and respect that the people under my covering can feel and see. However, it goes without saying that you cannot and will not please everyone. Some people simply have a contentious spirit and nothing you do will appease them. Honestly, some people don't come to church looking to be taught; they come looking for opportunities to teach, control others and exercise the evil that is in their hearts. When they do not get their way, they say that they've been hurt by the church when, in truth, they have hurt the church. So, it's important that we know when to call ourselves the victims and when to acknowledge that we are the victimizers.

Next, to heal from church hurt, you need to realize that the problem rests between you and a person or a group of people, meaning, it is not a problem between you and the Lord — unless you make it one. In other words, if you pull away from church altogether, you may be guilty of forsaking the coming together of the saints. This doesn't mean that you need to attend the same church that you were hurt or offended in; it simply means that you need to find a local church body to connect with.

Additionally, it is imperative that you continue to have a very active relationship with God, meaning, whether you are a part of a church body or not, you need to keep engaging God.

Isaiah 53:5 is one of my favorite scriptures and it reads, "But he was wounded for our transgressions, he was bruised for our iniquities: the chastisement of our peace was upon him; and with his stripes we are healed" (KJV). Vocabulary.com defines "chastisement" as: "The act of scolding or punishing someone." The aforementioned scripture speaks of the punishment that Jesus suffered in order that we may have peace. John 10:10 reads, "The thief cometh not, but for to steal, and to kill, and to destroy: I am come that they might have life, and that they might have it more abundantly." The Greek word for "abundance" is *perissos* and it is translated to mean: "(perí, "all-around, excess") – properly all-around, "more than" ("abundantly"); beyond what is anticipated, exceeding expectation; more abundant, going past the expected limit (Reference biblehub.com/ Strong's Concordance 4053). What does this mean for us? It means that Jesus suffered so that we may have more peace than what He had.

He died so that we could experience more than enough love, joy, peace and every good fruit that God has availed to His children. Jesus is the password to our peace: He is our divine access point, so to receive healing, we must first embrace that Jesus suffered so that we may have healing.

Next, we have to tell ourselves the truth. To reject this healing is the same as rejecting what the Lord has done for us. He didn't suffer through all that brutality only to have us crying that it's not enough. This means that you may not get the apology you want; you may never hear the people who hurt you acknowledge their wrongdoing and some doors that were shut as a result of what happened to you may remain shut. You have to make up your mind to be okay with that. There is no divine aura that's going to come upon you and force you to finally feel better about the situation. You have to choose to forgive; you have to choose to be happy, and you have to choose to move on. And then, you have to do something that makes even less sense; you have to make up your mind to forgive yourself. Some of the terrible feelings we experience after being rejected, betrayed, or persecuted are intensified towards others when we find ourselves angry at ourselves because of what we feel we allowed others to do to us. It's normal to wrestle with thoughts like, "I should have left the first time this happened," or "Why did I allow them to do what they did to me?" Oftentimes, we are more condemnatory toward ourselves than we are towards others. Self-correction is good, but self-condemnation is unhealthy and can lead to self-loathing, self-sabotage and fear of relationships. This is why it is just as important to forgive ourselves as it is for us to forgive others.

The next step to healing is to be honest with yourself about the situation. As you'll notice, throughout this book, I addressed many examples of perceived church hurt. In perceived church hurt, the self-proclaimed victim simply has a different view than that of the person or people he or she believes to have wronged him or her. I received quite a few submissions from people alleging to have been hurt by the church, but some of those submissions, I could not use because they were not examples of church hurt. For example, one of the most common offenses people report is being corrected by how they should address their leaders. Some people admittedly addressed their leaders by their first names and the leaders corrected them. To them, correction is not correction; it's a contentious confrontation when, in truth, it's not. It is disrespectful to address your leader or any person in authority by their first name. You wouldn't address an officer named Ben Williams as Ben. You'd either call him Officer Williams, Officer Ben or Mr. Williams. To call him Ben is disrespectful. It doesn't mean that he's being prideful or exalting himself; it simply means that you are respecting his office. The point is — you have to determine whether you are the one who's wrong or if you were truly wronged. To do this, ask yourself the following questions:

1. What led to the incident that hurt me? Sometimes, reviewing the story in your mind will help you to remember things you may have done or said that possibly sparked the incident.
2. What did I expect from the leader or congregant who hurt me? (Be honest with yourself.) What I've found is that expectation can be a weighty yoke and believers who

have not learned to cast their cares to the Lord will often try to cast all of their beliefs, problems and expectations on their leaders. For example, a woman may come to church every Sunday and Wednesday. Normally, she may be talkative and very engaged, but all of a sudden, she is silent. One day, the pastor receives her resignation letter and in it, she says, "You all know that I'm always the most talkative among you, but for three weeks, I came to service and I was quiet. I only had one person to ask me if anything was wrong; no one else seemed to care. For this reason, I do not believe that this is the church for me, so please accept my official resignation, effective immediately." The issue isn't that the leaders or the congregants did something wrong. The problem here is the woman had a set of personal beliefs that she thought were universal or should be universal. It would not be uncommon to hear that woman refer to her beliefs as "common sense," meaning, everyone should think that way. The truth is — she may have been so talkative that people were finally able to voice their opinions and questions once she stopped talking. People didn't like how talkative she was to begin with, so why would they try to start her up again? Sometimes, the issue is — both the offended and the offender have opposing beliefs and both people are immovable in regards to what they believe. Both people feel their views are "common sense" or better yet, unspoken laws that everyone should be abiding by.

3. Are my negative feelings about the situation centered around or fueled by something that happened to me before that incident? Let's say that Julia has never experienced what it's like to receive the protective love of a father. When Julia was young, her father stood by and did nothing when her mother attacked her, nor did he protect her from the many evil people in his family. For this reason, Julia was molested and abused as a young woman. However, Julia grows up and eventually gives her life to Christ. Now, this doesn't mean that Julia is upright; it means that she's started her ascension into the perfect will of God. One day, during bible study, Julia asks a

question that is considered by most of the congregants to be elementary. For this reason, Paula, one of the congregants decides to answer Julia. Paula isn't trying to be rude. The issue is that Julia wanted her pastor to answer, plus, she believes that Paula is simply showing off in front of the pastor. For this reason, Julia feels attacked, and she's even more hurt when the pastor does not address Paula's sudden urge to correct her. Julia sinks in her seat and remains quiet for the rest of the study, telling herself that she will never attend that church again. She says in her heart, "Pastor is just like my daddy. He doesn't care enough about me to protect me." Because of Julia's traumatic past and the fact that she hasn't healed from that past, it is easy for her to be offended. What offends her does not offend 99 percent of the congregants. In other words, the issue here isn't with the pastor, nor is it with Paula. The problem is that Julia needs to forgive her father. The point is — you need to make sure that you aren't filtering your present events by the events of your past. This is why Jesus said that we should not pour new wine into old wineskins. You cannot pour the issues of yesterday into the newness of today.

4. What am I guilty of doing to the person I believe to have wronged me? It is important that you intentionally look for areas where you may have been wrong. This helps you to avoid the victim mindset, whereas, you'll look at the situation through a subjective lens and not an objective one. In searching for your own errors, you may find that you did or said something that set off a chain of events — or maybe it was something you neglected to do or say. I'm not saying that the offending party is not guilty; I am saying that to move forward, you need to take accountability for anything you may have done or said.

People who are honest with themselves tend to have less physical and psychological issues than people who always see themselves as victims. Accountability is a powerful tool against the enemy; it separates the wise from the immature.

What if you can genuinely say that the problem was and is not you? Someone hurt you and that's the end of it. If this is the case, you need to forgive whomever it is that hurt you. I've learned the power of perspective; for example, I like to look at myself from another person's point of view. This doesn't mean that I'll agree with the person's perception of me; it simply means that I'm making an effort to understand that person. In many cases, you'll find that when you do this, it is easier to forgive the person. For example, you'll come across some people who you'll come to realize simply don't know any better. Sure, they know right from wrong, but they've been doing wrong for so long that it feels right to them. People like this usually hurt others and then, cast themselves as the victim. When you see this behavior, please know that the person has a lot of unresolved wounds on their souls and arguing with them or even being angry at them is pretty much the same as being contentiously involved with a four year old. I don't say that to be condescending; it's just one of the facts of life. Some people are so backed up with strife, jealousy, discord and the like that they can't go an entire week or an entire day without causing confusion or involving themselves in someone else's confusion. When we sow the energy of unforgiveness into such souls, we are simply joining a line-up of people who are, in a sense, their personal, but angry, servants. How is this? Any person you are mad at is your master; they have the ability to control the direction of your day. That's why God tells us to not let the sun go down on our wrath. For example, let's say that you were immensely angry with me. First, you would go out of your way to avoid me. This means that you would have to find out where I will be so that you won't go there, even if that means you miss a mighty move of God. Next, when you see me out, for example, at the supermarket, not only will you attempt to avoid me, but you'll start forgetting what you came there to get. This is because your anger or hatred towards me has become your superior emotion, so when it's flared up, everything else becomes secondary. Additionally, let's say that God promoted me and the news got to you that I'm now covering a hundred new churches, I've started a new clothing line and the Governor of North Carolina is scheduled to honor me in an upcoming event. This would further enrage you because, in your mind, you will feel as if God is rewarding me despite whatever it is you feel I've done to you. This anger would be especially intensified if you were struggling financially, emotionally and socially. This is why people find themselves getting angry with God. The problem isn't that the principles of sowing and reaping do not work; the problem is that they do work and they're working on them! For example, God told us that to attain His forgiveness, we have to forgive others. Nevertheless, some people feel that they are exempt from this rule and these feelings began to take root when they let the sun set on their wrath. In other words, they slept with their anger and now, they are one with it. For this reason, they will be haunted, misdirected and controlled by their hurt feelings. Whatever incident caused them to enter unforgiveness will become a picture on the wall of their memories. This is why it is necessary to forgive. Remember, forgiveness is not for them; it's for you.

If you've been done wrong by someone in the church, you need to take the incident and the memory of it and extract the wisdom from it. After that, toss that incident into the sea of forgetfulness.

I don't eat bones, so if a fish is in front of me, I know to extract the meat from the bones and toss the bones in the trash. There is meat in your pain, but you will only find it if you choose to forgive. Meat, in the scriptures, represents maturity, wisdom and having a full set of teeth. For example, babies can't chew steak because they don't have all of their teeth and they are not mature enough to understand that they need to thoroughly chew the steak. Instead, they'd try to swallow it and would end up choking. However, a mature adult has the teeth and the understanding they need to enjoy steak. The point is — what you take from the incident is a reflection of your spiritual age. Now, if you're not yet mature, the goal is to focus on maturing until you get to the point where every wrong that was done to you is no longer weighty enough to hinder you. Some people ask, "How do I forgive someone who's hurt me?" The answer is — grow past it. You won't go past it until you grow past it. Think of it this way — if a four year old little boy stepped on your foot at the supermarket but didn't apologize, you wouldn't make a big deal out of it. Why is this? Because he's a child and you are no longer on his level. You won't yell out, "Excuse you!" to a small child because you understand that foolishness is in the heart of a child. You'd let him walk by and the worst thing you may do is say in your heart that he needs discipline. However, let's say that the child's mother steps on your foot and she does not apologize. You will have a different reaction because you expect her to know better. She's an adult and as such, she knows that she's behaving rudely. Now, as you mature in Christ, you will even learn to excuse her because you'll soon come to understand that a person's physical age is not always a representation of that person's maturity level. She may be a very angry, contentious and frustrated woman who's void of wisdom. Howbeit, because you are wise, you know to not engage with her. Instead, you'd probably say "ouch" and watch her as she continued walking down the store's aisle. The reason you're not confronting her at this stage in your life is because you're no longer on the level she's on. You're no longer bound by pride and you weigh at the cost of a thing before you engage in it. You have no plans to be in the middle of a supermarket, fighting with some random woman, and then, escorted out of that supermarket in handcuffs. You have no plans to have your mugshot taken when you're not even sure why you're being arrested in the first place. Wisdom will tell you to overlook the offense and pray for her. Howbeit, if you're on her level, you won't be able to overlook it; you will feel the need to teach her a lesson. This means that if you felt, even now, as if you would want to avenge yourself, you need to study the scriptures about forgiveness and vengeance. You need to study the entire book of Proverbs until you grow past her. The same is true with church.

Grow past the incident; grow past the person or people who hurt you. To do this, you have to take your eyes and your focus off your pain and put it on Christ. The more you move forward in the Lord, the smaller the incident will appear to you. Sometimes, people stay angry because the person or people who hurt them have more influence than them. Sure, this is silly reasoning, but people commonly enter unforgiveness because they don't feel they have a big enough platform to address the lies and the rumors that are being spread about them. The truth is — you do not have to redeem yourself. In Job 19:25, Job says, "For I know that my Redeemer lives, and at the last he will stand upon the earth"

(ESV). Isaiah 54:5 says, "For your Maker is your husband, the LORD of hosts is his name; and the Holy One of Israel is your Redeemer, the God of the whole earth he is called" (ESV). Lastly, Psalm 78:35 reads, "And they remembered that God was their rock, and the high God their redeemer." Sometimes, the real problem isn't what happened to a person; it's that the person simply does not remember who his or her Redeemer is. This is why we need to search the scriptures daily so we can be reminded of our roles, responsibilities, and God's expectations of us, versus what we can expect from God. If you don't spend time with God on a daily basis, those lines will be blurred and you'll find yourself obsessing over problems that, quite frankly, you don't have the power or the resources to address. This means that should you try to address the problem, you will end up spending years trying to find a way to confront whatever problem or person you've allowed to become a Goliath in your life. And you can't address that issue in the name of the Lord if unforgiveness or vengeance is involved. Sometimes, you simply need to release people and trust that God will deal with them whenever and however He sees fit. One thing

I've found is that some people allow their anger to grow into bitterness and they expect the punishment for whomever it is that hurt them to be as harsh as their hatred towards that person. For example, let's say that I rebuked a young woman by the name of Jane Doe. In the span of a year, Jane has brought three men to church with her. These men are unrelated to Jane. As a matter of fact, she's entered the sanctuary holding hands with each of these men. So, one day, I tell Jane that there are young children in the church and I don't want them to think that her behavior is acceptable. I ask her to refrain from bringing her boyfriends to church; instead, she needs to focus on her relationship with Christ and whenever she gets engaged or married, she should definitely bring her fiancé or husband to church with her. Jane is offended by my request, but not because I'm being mean. The issue is that Jane keeps meeting seedy men, and then, bringing them to church hoping that they'll turn their lives around.

Offended, Jane reaches out to my superiors, hoping that they'll address me. As time progresses, Jane sees me continuously teaching and her anger turns to bitterness because her most recent boyfriend decided to end his relationship with her. After she tells him about the rebuke, Jane's new boyfriend sees an opportunity to end the relationship and he decides to use the church as his excuse. For this reason, she's not only angry at me for messing with her attempt to raise a man, she's now blaming me for her most recent breakup. Now, if my superiors were to address me, the worst they could say is for me to find a nicer way to convey my message from this point on, but because of the level of Jane's bitterness towards me, she wants me beheaded. Because beheading is illegal, she wants my superiors to sit me down and never allow me to preach again. If this doesn't happen, Jane would leave my church and proceed to attack my name and my character. After telling the story to a few people and seeing that they agree with me, Jane would feel the need to start adding lies to the story in her attempt to get people to agree with her. This is how anger works once it graduates to bitterness. An offended and bitter soul wants your punishment to be as great as their pain; this is why even after seeing the person or people who've offended them suffer, it is simply not enough to appease their wrath. Again, this is why we have to choose to forgive.

What if you're still attending the church where you were hurt? How can you continue to enter the sanctuary and see the person or people who've hurt you? First and foremost, if you were genuinely hurt and the person who wronged you is in leadership, my question to you is: why are you still going to that church? The most common response to such a question is, "God told me to stay." Obviously, if it is truly God who told you to stay, He told you to stay for a reason and that reason is not to expose the evils in that church. I have come across people who genuinely believe that their God-given assignment is to bring down churches and this is not true. This is why we need to test any voice that we hear that says that it is God. 1 John 4:1 warns us this way, "Beloved, do not believe every spirit, but test the spirits to see whether they are from God, for many false prophets have gone out into the world" (ESV). What this means is ... we need to make sure that we are hearing from God Himself and not some evil spirit pretending to be God. Remember 2 Corinthians 11:14, "No wonder, for even Satan disguises himself as an angel of light" (NASB). I'm not telling you that you are not hearing from God; what I am saying is test the spirit to make sure it's God.

If God told you to stay in a certain church, more than likely, the reason He wants you to stay is so that you can forgive the people there. Sometimes, God won't let us move on in the natural until we mentally and spiritually move on. This isn't to punish us. God does this to discipline us. Hebrews 12:6 says it this way, "For the Lord disciplines the one he loves, and chastises every son whom he receives." In other words, you may be holding yourself hostage at that church. Sometimes, we have to do the unthinkable and that is ... apologize to people who've done us wrong if, of course, they are offended with us. I know this makes absolutely no sense to the carnal mind, but remember, God's ways are not our ways. We want to do things one way when God says to do them another way. So, the reason God may require us to apologize is so we can truly wash our hands of the matter. This doesn't mean that your enemy has won; what it does mean is maybe God doesn't want you to see that person as your enemy. He wants you to see him or her as a fallen vessel who's desperately in need of mercy. Galatians 6:1 reads, "Brothers, if anyone is caught in any transgression, you who are spiritual should restore him in a spirit of gentleness. Keep watch on yourself, lest you too be tempted" (ESV). This scripture isn't just for the people who've sinned against others; it also applies to you restoring the people who've transgressed against you. In order to do this, you have to be spiritual and not carnal. In other words, you have to be led by the Spirit of God. Galatians 5:22-24 tells us what the fruit of the Spirit looks like. It reads, "But the fruit of the Spirit is love, joy, peace, patience, kindness, goodness, faithfulness, gentleness, self-control; against such things there is no law. And those who belong to Christ Jesus have crucified the flesh with its passions and desires" (ESV). The book of Galatians also tells us what the fruit of the flesh looks like. Galatians 5:19-21 reads, "Now the works of the flesh are evident: sexual immorality, impurity, sensuality, idolatry, sorcery, enmity, strife, jealousy, fits of anger, rivalries, dissensions, divisions, envy, drunkenness, orgies, and things like these. I warn you, as I warned you before, that those who do such things will not inherit the kingdom of God" (ESV).

As you can see, strife, dissension, fits of anger, rivalries, and enmity are strongholds of the flesh and we are commanded to not be led by them. Again, if you truly forgive the offense, God may send you to a new church where you'll finally join the church body that God has assigned you to become one with.

As long as you're in the church where you were hurt, be loving, kind, forgiving and most of all — patient. You may have to forgive that same person time and time again until you learn to master loving others.

Lastly, there are many cases where people stay at the wrong churches because they're too afraid to move on. They're afraid that the people at their former church will rejoice and talk about them when or if they leave, so they stay. For this reason, they become more and more bitter with each visit to their churches. If you tell them they should leave, they would only say, "God told me to stay here." God didn't tell them that. If you want to know if God told you to go or leave, check your motives. If God tells you to stay, it won't make any sense to you whatsoever. If it's your flesh telling you to stay, you will think of a few reasons that you should stay; for example, you may say, "I don't want them to win, after all, I know they are trying to drive me out of this church" or "I need to clear my name." These are all flesh issues that can be resolved if you would only trust God and stop being led by your flesh. God told us that vengeance belongs to Him and Him only. Clearing your name is not your job; it's God's job.

Remember to continue to live in love towards others, despite what people say or do to you. In this life, we will be hurt, judged and unfairly persecuted, but it's all a part of the price we pay for loving and serving the Lord. If you're willing to pay the price, pay it, but don't lose the fruit of the Spirit in the process. Let people be the imperfect beings that they are and do for them what God has done for you: forgive them, and remember, not everyone understands what they're doing — including some leaders. It was the Pharisees who wanted Jesus crucified; these were leaders in the Jewish church. However, Jesus asked God to forgive them, citing one of His most famous lines and that is, "Father, forgive them, for they know not what they do" (Luke 23:24). If Jesus could forgive a multitude of people who not only followed, harassed, spat on, whipped and eventually killed Him; we should be able to forgive the few folks who've talked about, ignored, rejected, lied on or laughed at us. Always remind yourself that the price tag of righteousness is pretty high, and then ask yourself this very important question, "Am I willing to pay this price or would I much rather stay comfortable my entire life?" Remember Mark 13:13, which reads, "And you will be hated by all for my name's sake. But the one who endures to the end will be saved" (ESV). Also remember Matthew 5:11; it reads, "Blessed are you when others revile you and persecute you and utter all kinds of evil against you falsely on my account" (ESV). This means that in being blessed, we must accept the good with the bad. Again, forgive the people who hurt you and move at the speed of love. Forgiveness is a branch of love and if you hold on to it, you will find yourself growing to new heights in Christ Jesus.

Speak the below prayer, but before you do, determine within your heart and your mind to

Healing from Church Hurt

forgive the person or people who've hurt or angered you. One facet of forgiveness is accepting that despite what was done to you, God may still turn around and bless the folks who hurt you. This isn't to reward them; it's to demonstrate to them what true, godly love looks like. Sometimes, He does this to help us to see exactly where we are in the forgiveness process. If we're still offended, we'll get angry when we see our enemies blessed, but if we've truly forgiven them, we won't be bothered by it. Lastly, I think God does this to show us how He wants us to love on our enemies. Understand this — when you love and bless someone who doesn't deserve it, you are acting just like Father God. After all, He loves and blesses us, despite what we've put Him through.

Remind yourself that you are a branch of the Tree of Life, Jesus Christ, and you get to determine what grows on the tree of your life — whether it be the fruit of the Holy Spirit or the fruit of the flesh. Also remind yourself that all fruits will attract pests, nevertheless, if you stay submitted to Christ, they won't be able to uproot or harm you in any way. Luke 10:19 says this of you, "Behold, I have given

you authority to tread on serpents and scorpions, and over all the power of the enemy, and nothing shall hurt you." (ESV). Psalms 1:1-6 reads, "Blessed is the man
who walks not in the counsel of the wicked,
nor stands in the way of sinners, nor sits in the seat of scoffers; but his delight is in the law of the Lord, and on his law he meditates day and night. He is like a tree planted by streams of water that yields its fruit in its season, and its leaf does not wither. In all that he does, he prospers. The wicked are not so, but are like chaff that the wind drives away. Therefore the wicked will not stand in the judgment, nor sinners in the congregation of the righteous; for the Lord knows the way of the righteous, but the way of the wicked will perish."

Prayer

Father God, I come before you asking that you forgive me for all of my sins. Lord, I confess this day to you that I am unworthy of your love and your forgiveness, but yet, you still give it to me. Lord, I ask you to help me extend to the people who've hurt me, the same grace you've extended to me time and time again. I ask that you visit the hearts of

everyone who's hurt me and teach them to love your people the way that you love them. Father, I stand in the gap for others who have been wounded in the church and I ask that you help them to forgive, love and move forward. Lord, I ask that you arrest the spirits of division and offense that the enemy has sent out against the church and restore your people yet again. Teach us to love one another despite our flaws. Help us to walk together in unity and help us to see the big picture so that we can press towards the mark of the higher calling. Father, I ask that you heal churches, communities and families and help us to walk together as one person so that your name will be glorified. I give you my hurt, offense, and hatred, and I ask that you give me your peace, grace and love in return. It is in Jesus name that I pray.
Amen.

Made in the USA
Columbia, SC
08 March 2021